The Library of World Biography

Bolívar

Donald E. Worcester

THE LIBRARY OF WORLD BIOGRAPHY
J. H. PLUMB, GENERAL EDITOR

Little, Brown and Company — Boston – Toronto

FIRST EDITION

T05/77

LIBRARY OF CONGRESS CATALOGING IN PUBLICATION DATA

Worcester, Donald Emmet, 1915–
  Bolívar.

  (The Library of world biography)
  Bibliography: p.
  Includes index.
  1. Bolívar, Simón, 1783–1830.   2. Heads of state—
South America—Biography.   3. South America—History—
Wars of Independence, 1806–1830.
F2235.3.W67   980'.2'0924 [B]   76–56616
ISBN 0–316–95390–3

Published simultaneously in Canada
by Little, Brown & Company (Canada) Limited

PRINTED IN THE UNITED STATES OF AMERICA

Introduction

WHEN WE LOOK back at the past nothing, perhaps, fascinates us so much as the fate of individual men and women. The greatest of these seem to give a new direction to history, to mold the social forces of their time and create a new image, or open up vistas that humbler men and women never imagined. An investigation of the interplay of human temperament with social and cultural forces is one of the most complex yet beguiling studies a historian can make: men molded by time, and time molded by men. It would seem that to achieve greatness both the temperament and the moment must fit like a key into a complex lock. Or rather like a master key, for the very greatest of men and women resonate in ages distant to their own. Later generations may make new images of them — one has only to think what succeeding generations of Frenchmen have made of Napoleon, or Americans of Benjamin Franklin — but this only happens because some men change the course of history and stain it with their own ambitions, desires, creations or hopes of a magnitude that embraces future generations like a miasma. This is particularly true of the great figures of religion, of politics, of war. The great creative spirits, however, are used by subsequent generations in a reverse manner — men and women go to them to seek hope or solace, or to confirm despair, reinterpreting the works of imagination or wisdom to ease them in their own desperate necessities, to beguile them with a sense of beauty or merely to draw from them strength and understanding. So this series of biographies tries in lucid, vivid, and dramatic narratives to explain the greatness of men and women — not only how they managed to secure their niche in the great pantheon of Time, but also why they have continued to fascinate subsequent generations. It may seem, therefore, that it is paradoxical for this series to contain living men and women, as well as the dead, but it is not so. We can recognize, in our own time, particularly in those whose careers are getting close to their final hours, men and women of indisputable greatness, whose position in history is secure, and about whom the legends and myths are beginning to sprout — for all great men and women become legends, all become in history larger than their own lives.

The success of the American Revolution had alarming repercussions upon its great allies France and Spain, without whose support independence might have been more difficult to achieve. Spain, indeed, had entered the war in order to strengthen her power in America. Her aim was not only to recover West Florida, which she accomplished, but also to turn the British out of Jamaica, which proved impossible. Nevertheless, strategically and materially, Spain emerged from the conflict with Britain far stronger than she had been in the 1770s. Yet within fifty years, her empire, which stretched from Tierra del Fuego to San Francisco, was in ruins, indeed broken into enduring fragments. The claims that she had long made on Central and

North America became a hollow farce, treated with contempt by white settlers from the eastern states.

Simón Bolívar was as responsible as anyone for the breakup of the Spanish Empire; indeed, he was the greatest man produced by Colonial Spain. He was very much a child of the Enlightenment, bred on a diet of Rousseau and Voltaire. He studied avidly the Declaration of Independence and greatly admired Jefferson. Like Lafayette, he was a romantic aristocrat. His imagination was made almost drunk by the name of Liberty — Liberty, however, that he never bothered to define; for Bolívar was a man of action, not a man of reflection. Ultimately, Liberty to him was little more than the rejection of Old Spain. Toward that ideal, at least, he showed endurance, absolute dedication, brilliant improvisation, and a capacity to stir the aspirations of the Spanish colonists and to hold their loyalty. Not all of them all of the time. He was too erratic for that. But no matter how dark his prospects — and they were often pitch-black — he could always arouse some support. And in the end he attracted enough men to win. Bolívar had much of the color, the dramatic sense of a Garibaldi, and he proved to be a superb man of action. He failed in statesmanship. Whether or not a federal system might have worked in Spanish America is arguable, but the result of independence was certainly predictable. Independence was followed by a century of murderous wars, bloody coups, and cruel dictatorships. These events cannot be blamed on Bolívar, although a different type of revolutionary — one more systematic, more orthodox, more concerned for structures of government — might have achieved more. But the situation in the Spanish colonies was more productive of Bolívars than of Franklins or Adamses. The mercantile class was small and not of great significance, whereas the landowners and the royal state officials dominated Spanish colonial society. Their attitude toward life was aristocratic, no matter how inferior they might have felt in the presence of the nobility of Old Spain. So, like feudal barons, they fought for liberties rather than Liberty. They may have venerated the Declaration of Independence, but — as with the Southern planters — for them the application of its message was limited.

And yet, America's example certainly made Bolívar's success possible — that and the Revolution in France, which hamstrung an already enfeebled Spain. Nor should we forget that once it was unleashed the struggle for Spanish-American independence provided a fertile ground for the war-hungry, half-pay officers of Wellington's army; without them, victory might have proved more difficult. Bolívar's name and reputation resonated in Europe as well as in the Americas. And it has continued to do so, for Bolívar remains, like Byron, one of the great symbols of romantic nationalism. And like Byron, his private life lived up to his public image — as vital in the boudoir as on the battlefield.

—J. H. PLUMB

Contents

Prologue

THE SPANISH-AMERICAN COLONIES were established when Europe was at the threshold of the era of modern nation-states. Society was still largely medieval in outlook, divided into corporations such as the guilds, the Church, the nobles, and the universities, each independent of the others and jealous of its *fueros,* or privileges. Cooperation among the different corporations to achieve a common goal was rare — each looked to a powerful monarch to protect it against unjust treatment. As Spaniards knew, the king was just, but his officials might not be. Spaniards felt free, therefore, to rebel against unfair officials without considering themselves in opposition to the king. Rebellions in the Spanish tradition customarily began with the shout: "Long live the king! Death to bad government!" Most of the Spanish-American revolutions began with vivas for Ferdinand VII — only the small group of plotters for independence knew where the movements would end.

If Columbus had sailed for Henry VII of England (as he offered to do), the culture traits that the English colonists would have brought to the New World would not have been vastly different from those brought by Spaniards in the late fifteenth century. By 1600, however, there had been fundamental changes in northern Europe and in Britain, particularly owing to the Reformation. The ideas of Luther and Calvin created a new outlook, especially with regard to education, the self-government of congregations, individual decision-making, and so forth; and this outlook was able to operate freely in the North American wilderness. There no entrenched nobility, peasantry, or priesthood was present to raise obstacles to change. Spaniards and Spanish Americans remained faithful to the concept of authority in religion and government, while Anglo-Americans gravitated toward a belief in reason and individual opinion.

Spain did not introduce the typical feudal relationships and duties into her colonies, although manorialism, the economic basis for feudalism, did spread throughout Spanish America (where land, rather than money, is still the hallmark of quality). Without feudalism, ownership of land or of other forms of wealth did not carry with it political, judicial, and military responsibilities. Because wealthy and able Creoles were generally excluded from positions of trust in church and state, they failed to develop a sense of civic responsibility, and their ingrained irresponsibility did not miraculously vanish when they and their countrymen fought for independence from Spain. Spanish-American aristocrats did not regard the feudal bond between property and civic responsibility as a natural condition, for each considered himself above the law. Spanish colonial officials early devised a way of handling those royal decrees that would have aroused resentment or rebellion. Holding such decrees, they would say, "I obey but do not comply."

Another aspect of the Spanish tradition that affected

Spanish Americans was the fundamental dichotomy be-tween those for whom liberty was the greatest goal and those who valued efficiency above all else. Liberty, when pursued to its logical conclusion, resulted in anarchy; effi-ciency, when carried to the extreme, produced tyranny. There was not, as Bolívar learned, a workable compromise between the two attitudes, though he devoted much of his life to seeking one. He labored to create a system that would preserve unity and stability through a powerful, centralized government while retaining as much individ-ual liberty as possible; but his efforts were both exhausting and fruitless.

Venezuela, where Bolívar's revolutionary career began, is divided into four distinct geographic regions. The northern highlands are composed of a branch of the An-dean chain that enters western Venezuela and runs north-eastward to near the coast, then eastward toward the island of Trinidad, except for a gap in the Barcelona region. The Maracaibo lowlands lie along the Venezuelan-Colombian border and include Lake Maracaibo, a shallow body of water one hundred twenty miles long and about half as wide. The third major region is the Orinoco Llanos, an area of vast plains that slope gradually from the base of the Andes to the Río Orinoco. South of the Río Orinoco are the Guiana Highlands, which make up about half of Venezuelan territory.

Caracas, the capital, lies in a mountain basin extending about fifteen miles east and west and separated from the port of La Guaira by a low range of mountains. To the west, the basin of Valencia has been the most productive agricultural area since early times. It is surrounded by mountains, but low passes give easy access to both the llanos to the south and Puerto Cabello to the west.

The Orinoco Llanos are grasslands six hundred miles

long and two hundred miles wide that have supported enormous herds of cattle since the mid-sixteenth century. Because of extreme variations between flood and drought, it is not ideal grazing country; although torrential rains inundate it from June to October, from January through March it is so dry that most of the streams disappear. In the rainy season the herds must be driven to higher ground between Calabozo and Valencia. During the months of drought they are driven to the wet regions near the Río Orinoco. The native grasses are so low in nutritional value that the cattle are close to starvation most of the year. The llanos are also plagued by a rich variety of stinging, disease-carrying insects that increase the misery of both man and beast. When the independence struggles began, there were between four million and five million head of cattle on the llanos, but by 1820, owing to the inroads of royalist and patriot armies, fewer than three hundred thousand remained.

New Granada (or modern Colombia) is thoroughly fragmented by four Andean ranges separated by deep chasms, making east-west travel difficult. The western third of the country is composed of mountains and valleys. The eastern two-thirds form part of the Guiana Highlands and the Orinoco Llanos.

In 1810 Venezuela's population was less than one million, composed of about twenty percent white; sixty percent Negroes and *pardos,* or mixed-bloods of brown skin; and the rest Indians and mestizos, or half-breeds. A small group of aristocrats — less than one percent of the population — owned most of the land. Class consciousness was sharpened by their fear of the *pardos,* on the one hand, and, on the other, by their resentment against Spanish officials for policies that excluded these aristocrats from high office. Fear of the *pardos'* gaining control turned the landowners against most attempts at rebellion.

It was in this milieu that Simón Bolívar was born and reared, and that his outlook was formed. Although he was able to rise above the intellectual and social limitations of time and place, few of his contemporaries were able to follow his example.

ONE

The Making of a Rebel

IN THE LAST year of the eighteenth century Venezuelan Simón Bolívar played battledore and shuttlecock with the prince of Asturias, future Ferdinand VII, before the royal court in Madrid. During the game Bolívar accidentally knocked the prince's hat from his head. Ferdinand, scion of the absolutist Spanish Bourbons, expected an apology, but none was forthcoming from the seventeen-year-old Creole aristocrat. They later met again, not face to face, in a war to the death as Bolívar battled the Spanish Empire for the independence of his native land. Years later, recalling the game in Madrid, Bolívar asked, "Who would have prophesied to Ferdinand VII that this was a sign that one day I might tear the costliest jewel from his crown?"

The Bolívars, descendants of a noble Basque family, were among the elite of Caracas almost from the founding of the city in 1567. An ancestor, Simón de Bolívar, had been chosen in 1589 to represent the city in Spain and he remained there until 1592. Caracas, located in the heart of a fertile valley, possesses one of the most attractive settings of any New World capital. In the late eighteenth century it was the third largest city in Spanish South America, and one of the most prosperous. The province of Caracas contained about half of Venezuela's people.

In an era when Spaniards were obsessed with *limpieza de sangre* (purity of blood), meaning no non-Christians among one's forebears, Bolívar's ancestors included only one doubtful member. His great-grandmother, María Petronila de Ponte, was illegitimate, and although in his will her father declared her mother to be his equal in birth, there were no records to confirm this claim. Creoles were people of European ancestry born in the Americas, and since few Spanish women came to the New World in the early years, many of the leading "Creole" families had Indians or Africans lurking somewhere in the family tree, and the king used this "tainted" blood as justification for excluding them from positions of trust. The treatment of Creoles as inferior to *Peninsulares* — Spaniards born in Spain — was a long-standing cause of frustration and resentment that contributed to the desire for independence.

Simón José Antonio de la Trinidad Bolívar y Palacios was born on July 24, 1783, the year England's North American colonies won their independence. He was the fourth child of Juan Vicente Bolívar and Doña María de la Concepción de Palacios y Blanco, who already had two daughters, María Antonia and Juana María, and a son, Juan Vicente. Simón was only three when his father died, and nine when his mother succumbed to tuberculosis in 1792. Soon after this his grandfather died and his sisters married, so he grew up without close family ties. Years later he instructed one of his sisters to treat his Negro nurse, Hipolita, as if she were their own mother. "She nourished my life," he wrote. "I know no other parent than her."

Simón's father had been an important figure, the possessor of twelve houses in Caracas and La Guaira, herds of cattle, indigo plantations, mines, and the San Mateo sugar plantation that had been in the family for at least two centuries. He had organized a militia battalion in which his youngest son would later serve, and he had been Caracas's deputy to Madrid for five years. Like many Creoles who visited Spain, he was badly disillusioned by Spain's backwardness in comparison to other European nations.

Dissatisfaction with Spanish rule, and especially with the trade monopoly given the Guipúzcoa (or Caracas) Company earlier, was intensified by the knowledge that the kings of Spain and France had helped the English colonies win independence. It seems likely that neither court reflected long or seriously on the contagious nature of revolutions, for both France and Spain had actually fought against Britain rather than for the Anglo-American colonists. Spanish-American Creoles ignored this distinction. In September, 1780, Intendant José de Abalos warned Minister of the Indies José de Gálvez about the trade monopoly and the anger it aroused. "The woeful and rancorous tone of their laments increases daily," he said,

> and unless His Majesty grants them the open trade for which they sigh they will lend their ears and hearts to any hint and help offered them by the Crown's enemies. . . . This is not an empty prophecy, but the forecast of one who knows this country well; and if this part of America is lost it will be the most lamentable misfortune for the monarchy . . . because with this gate in his power he who possesses it will easily absorb the rest of the continent. He who dominates the provinces of Caracas and Cumaná and the island of Trinidad will be master of this whole western region, and with it he will have easy access to the rest.

In July of the following year, Simón's father and other Creole aristocrats wrote to Francisco de Miranda, Venezu-

THE MAKING OF A REBEL 〜 11

ela's "precursor" of independence. "We find ourselves in a shameful prison, and are treated worse than the Negro slaves whose masters trust them more. We have no choice but to throw off this unbearable and disgraceful yoke." Had he lived longer the senior Bolívar might well have participated in the struggle to which his son devoted his life. "At the first sign from you," he and his friends told Miranda, "we are ready to follow you as our leader to the very end, and to shed the last drop of our blood in this great and honorable undertaking." Miranda thought it wise to wait until the Anglo-American colonies had achieved their independence, "which was bound to be in the future the infallible preliminary of ours."

After the death of his parents and his grandfather, Simón was still exposed to the best teachers available, including Andrés Bello, only three years his senior, and Simón Rodríguez, whose biographer aptly entitled his study *Genius or Madman?* Simón Carreño, alias Rodríguez, wanted to live as an eighteenth-century "natural man" or child of nature. He was widely read in the philosophies of Spinoza, Holbach, and especially Rousseau; and he appears to have had a lasting influence on young Bolívar, even though his pupil was not of scholarly bent. Later Bolívar admitted to him, "You have molded my heart for liberty and justice — for the great and the beautiful."

Venezuelans displayed an interest in independence and republicanism in 1797 when Spain exiled some republican agitators to Venezuela, where they were imprisoned in La Guaira, presumably to rot in harmless seclusion. But many merchants, mestizos, and artisans sympathized with them, and they were able to enlist prominent men such as José María de España and Manuel Gual in a republican plot. The prisoners were released and were helped out of the country, but the republican revolution was betrayed. Most of the conspirators were arrested, for they advocated racial equality as well as the abolition of slavery and Indian tribute. Threatened by such radical goals, the wealthy aristocrats supported the government. Some of the same men who had signed the letter to Miranda in 1781 were among the first to offer their services to the government. Gual escaped, but España was captured and executed along with others, despite Charles IV's secret order to the Audiencia judges to avoid severe measures and not to treat as crimes what might be only the result of "seduction and ignorance." Simón Rodríguez was arrested but released because of lack of evidence. Not waiting for such evidence to appear, he left the country. This episode made it clear that the Caracas aristocrats wanted independence only on their own terms and under their complete control, preferring rule by Spain to that by lower-class Venezuelans.

Pablo Vizcardo, one of the Jesuits expelled from Spanish America in 1767, wrote a letter, which was published in French in Philadelphia in 1799, urging Spanish Americans to rebel. He reminded Spanish Americans of the successful American Revolution: "The valor with which the English colonies of America have fought for liberty, which they now gloriously enjoy, fills our own indolence with shame. We have yielded to them the palm with which they . . . have crowned the New World with an independent sovereignty. Add to it the interest with which the courts of Spain and France have backed the cause of the English Americans. Let all that be a stimulus for our honor provoked by so many insults during three hundred years." Miranda distributed copies of this letter widely over South America.

In 1799 Simón was sent to Madrid to be with relatives who presumably could secure him some preferment at court. His uncle Esteban Palacios saw at once that he lacked certain knowledge and social graces, and had him instructed in languages, mathematics, dancing, and dueling. Although he was being trained for the intellectually shallow life of a courtier, Bolívar finally acquired a zest for reading.

The tone of the Spanish court at this time was set by Charles IV, Queen María Luisa, and their mutual friend and benefactor Manuel de Godoy. The "Prince of Peace" served both monarchs — Charles as a cabinet minister, and María Luisa in a more intimate office. The court, reflecting the unconventional behavior of the royal family, inspired no more respect in the young Venezuelan than it did among Europeans. Bolívar developed not only deep scorn for Spanish rulers but a hatred of monarchy as well. It was at this time he played the symbolic game of battledore and shuttlecock with the future Ferdinand VII.

For a time Bolívar lived at the home of the Marqués de Ustariz, where he met and courted María Teresa, daughter of Venezuelan Bernardo Rodríguez de Toro, brother of the Marqués de Toro. Because she was three years older than seventeen-year-old Bolívar, her father and the Marqués de Ustariz insisted the wedding be postponed.

Owing perhaps to Bolívar's acquaintance with Manuel Mallo, a former favorite of the queen, he was one day handed an order from the minister of finance concerning his excessive use of diamonds; the queen apparently had ordered the search to see if Bolívar carried love letters from Mallo to other women. Sword in hand, Bolívar refused to submit to the search. Friends interceded and prevented serious trouble for him, but he left Madrid immediately; after visiting his future wife and her family in Bilbao, he went on to Paris.

When he returned to Spain in mid-1802, the young couple married and sailed for La Guaira. They lived happily in Caracas for less than a year before María Teresa died of a fever. Grief-stricken, Bolívar vowed never to remarry — a vow he kept. (He did not, however, vow chastity.) He remarked later that if his wife had lived he would not have taken up the struggle for independence. "My wife's death," he said, "led me early in my career onto the road of politics."

One of the wealthiest men in Caracas, Bolívar was always indifferent to money, equally willing to share it with others or to squander it. He sailed for Cádiz, and after visiting María Teresa's father, joined a group of wealthy young Spanish Americans in Madrid. They reinforced his resentment of Spaniards' treatment of Creoles as inferior. When the government used the excuse of a temporary food shortage to send all "foreigners" out of Madrid, Bolívar journeyed to Paris, where he was reunited with his former tutor Simón Rodríguez. He also renewed his acquaintance with Fanny Dervieu du Villars, whom he had met at his wife's home in Bilbao. They decided on rather insecure evidence that they were cousins, and Bolívar took an apartment in her home. Her husband, Baron Dervieu du Villars, an officer in the Napoleonic army, was often away. At Fanny's salon Bolívar met many prominent French military and political officials, and Fanny was one of many who would help alleviate his marital sorrow.

Among the important figures Bolívar met at this time was the much-traveled Prussian scientist Alexander von Humboldt, who arrived in France in 1804 after five years on a scientific expedition to South America. They discussed Venezuela, a land Humboldt considered ripe for an independence movement. "But," he told the future Liberator, "I cannot see the man who is to achieve it." Aimé Bompland, the young Frenchman who had accompanied Humboldt, was more optimistic. "Revolutions themselves," he said, "bring forth great men who are worthy of carrying them out," and he encouraged Bolívar.

Bolívar was much impressed by Napoleon's stunning

military successes, but he regarded Napoleon's self-crowning in December, 1804, a betrayal of the republic. "He became emperor," Bolívar said, "and from that day I regarded him as a hypocritical tyrant." As he saw Napoleon the center of attention and admiration, however, Bolívar developed a burning desire to emulate him. "Freedom and fame" became his motto and goal in life.

In Paris Simón Rodríguez employed Rousseau's works in an effort to counteract Napoleon's influence on Bolívar. When, twenty years later, a friend gave Bolívar the copy of Rousseau's *Contrat Sociale* that Napoleon had read on St. Helena, it became one of his most prized possessions, one he willed to his native city.

In 1805, when Napoleon announced his intention of going to Milan to be crowned king of Italy, Bolívar and Rodríguez set out for Italy, walking much of the way. In Rome they met Humboldt again, and once more discussed Spanish-American independence. One day Rodríguez and Bolívar climbed the Monte Sacro, recalling the Roman plebs who had fled there to escape oppression by the patricians. The patrician Bolívar, emotionally aroused by thoughts of freedom and oppression, knelt, clasped his companion's hands, and vowed to liberate his homeland.

News of Bolívar's vow spread quickly among Spaniards living in Rome, but few believed he was serious. The Spanish ambassador presented Bolívar to Pope Pius VII; an embarrassing moment followed, for Bolívar refused to kiss the cross on the pope's sandal. Pius tactfully solved the awkward problem by extending his ring. Bolívar commented afterward that "the Pope must hold the symbol of Christianity very cheap, if he wears it on his shoes, whereas the proudest princes of Christendom wear it on their crowns."

Back in Paris Bolívar discussed his intentions with friends, and his plans began to take shape. He did not underestimate the difficulties ahead, for he knew that Spain would not relinquish her empire without a struggle. At this time he learned of Miranda's landing on the Venezuelan coast in an abortive attempt to arouse the people to rebellion.

Francisco de Miranda had been born in Caracas in 1750. His father was from the Canary Islands, and because he was a merchant, Creole aristocrats resented his financing the formation of a militia company of which Spanish officials named him captain. They harassed him into resigning his commission. Perhaps the unfriendly atmosphere in Caracas induced young Francisco to go to Spain and purchase a captaincy in the Spanish army. While in Spain he inquired concerning his ancestors, and learned that his family's coat of arms had five half bodies of maidens on a red field, which, as Salvador de Madariaga wryly commented, "considering the lifelong record of Miranda in the field of maidens, would appear to show that wit and hazard can meet."

In 1780 Miranda was sent to Cuba, where he joined the expedition that recovered Pensacola from the British. He later got into difficulties, and one month before Bolívar was born he evaded arrest and fled to the United States. It was at this time that he became obsessed with the idea of liberating Venezuela and the rest of Spanish America.

In advising young Spanish Americans concerning the methods of achieving independence, Miranda urged them to emulate the American rather than the French Revolution. Both revolutionary groups had excellent slogans, and the French, particularly during the Terror, actually put some of their slogans into effect. But Anglo-American rebels, while loftily declaring that all men were created equal, were in fact led and governed by Creole slave owners such as George Washington and Thomas Jefferson. This situation appealed to pseudo-aristocrat Miranda as well as to Creole plantation owners in general. They wanted simply to replace the *Peninsulares* at the apex of society and government, without disturbing the castes and classes beneath them. What they found appropriate in the American Declaration of Independence was that certain rights were "unalienable," and "that whenever any form of government becomes destructive of these ends, it is the right of the people to alter or to abolish it, and to institute new government."

Miranda traveled all over Europe, talking to men and making love to women, and keeping records of both activities. Catherine the Great gave him a commission in the Russian army, which he apparently earned through services more social than martial. In France he served in the revolutionary armies, rising to the rank of brigadier general. He tried repeatedly to persuade the British to help liberate his country, holding out favorable trade concessions as bait.

In 1805 Napoleon cowed Charles IV and Godoy into lending him most of the Spanish navy for use against England, and they paid him an annual indemnity for the same purpose. On October 21 Lord Nelson destroyed the combined French-Spanish fleet off Cape Trafalgar. Spain still had a few warships in the Caribbean and off the Pacific coast of South America, but Nelson's classic victory meant that France would be unable to help Spain hold or reconquer her American colonies. The weakening of the Spanish navy encouraged Miranda to plan an invasion of Venezuela by sea. Late in 1805 he sailed to the United States, where friendly merchants helped him obtain a small vessel, the *Leander,* and to recruit a small force as the nucleus of his army.

Spanish officials in the United States learned of his plans and alerted royal officials in Caracas in time for them to make preparations. After costly delays Miranda tried twice to initiate a rebellion in Venezuela, but failed miserably and was forced to seek the protection of British warships. Among those who joined the forces opposing Miranda were two who would later participate in the struggle for independence — Juan Vicente Bolívar and the Marqués de Toro. The Creole aristocrats of Caracas still opposed any movement they did not control.

After his dismal failure Miranda returned to London, where he persuaded Sir Arthur Wellesley, later Duke of Wellington, to assemble a force of 13,000 men in Ireland for the liberation of Venezuela. But before the expedition could sail French troops had invaded Portugal to impose Napoleon's "Continental System" and close all European ports to British commerce. In their march across northern Spain the French garrisoned all fortified cities. The Portuguese royal family, protected by British warships, sailed for Brazil as French artillery could be heard on the outskirts of Lisbon.

In 1806 the British sent two expeditions to "liberate" Buenos Aires. The Spanish viceroy fled, but the Argentine Creoles, led by a French officer in the Spanish service, drove the British out on both occasions. Having defeated troops that had served against Napoleon's armies, the Creoles were convinced that their supposed "inferiority" to Peninsular Spaniards was a fabrication. Their victories gave a tremendous boost to Creole morale and encouraged those who plotted the various independence movements. Bolívar returned to Venezuela in 1807 and began actively promoting independence.

Charles IV, seeing Napoleon's shadow looming over Spain, sought to emulate the Portuguese rulers by seeking a haven in the New World. He had reached Aranjuez on his way south when an uprising of Ferdinand's followers caused him to abdicate in favor of his son. Early in 1808 Napoleon persuaded Charles and María Luisa to come to

Bayonne, and soon after this Ferdinand also journeyed to Bayonne, despite the fact that the people of Valladolid cut the traces of his carriage mules in an effort to prevent his leaving Spain.

Napoleon forced Ferdinand to abdicate in favor of his father, and Charles to step down in favor of Napoleon's brother Joseph, king of Naples. Although Spaniards would later realize that Joseph was far superior to Ferdinand as a monarch, they resented Napoleon's interference, and they remained loyal to their legitimate king, Ferdinand the Desired. On May 2, 1808 (*dos de mayo*), the Spanish people, without army or king, took an audacious step no other European people had dared to take — guerrilla warfare against Napoleon's all-conquering armies. It was in the Peninsular campaigns that Napoleon's downfall began, for not only were his armies eventually driven from Spain and Portugal, but other European peoples took heart and tried to emulate the courageous Spaniards and Portuguese.

After the *dos de mayo* uprising in Madrid, Sir Arthur Wellesley's Venezuela expedition was diverted to Portugal and Spain, to enter the campaigns against the French. Wellesley had the unpleasant duty of informing Miranda of this disappointing change of plan. Knowing Miranda's excitable nature, Wellesley chose to break the bad news in public on a street, hoping to prevent a violent outburst. "But even there he was so loud and angry," Wellesley reported, "that I told him I would walk on first a little that we might not attract the notice of everybody passing. When I joined him again later he was cooler." Miranda's disappointment can easily be imagined, for his most cherished dream was blasted just at the point of fulfillment.

Doubting that Joseph could maintain the Spanish Empire intact, Napoleon hoped to swing the Spanish colonies to France and away from Britain. He therefore sent agents to the Spanish colonies, encouraging them in their desire for independence and assuring them of France's friendship.

News that the French had invaded Spain reached Caracas from Trinidad in mid-1808, but neither royalists nor Creoles believed the reports. In July, however, a French ship anchored at La Guaira with Napoleon's agents aboard. Venezuelans now learned that Joseph Bonaparte was king of Spain, and that the Spanish people were in rebellion against France. Royal officials were perturbed and tried to keep the news secret, for the legitimacy of their authority had vanished with the abdication of Ferdinand and Charles.

Here was an unexpected opportunity for the Creoles, for by rejecting the usurper Joseph and proclaiming loyalty to Ferdinand they could undercut the authority of all royal officials, many of whom were quite willing to accept Joseph in order to maintain their own positions. While Creoles noisily declared their allegiance to Ferdinand the Desired, Napoleon's emissaries fled for their lives. It made no difference to Creole plotters that Ferdinand had only one desirable attribute — his absence from Spain; he gave them an opportunity to set in motion a movement for independence without betraying their ultimate intentions.

Each major Spanish city created juntas, or councils of government, to rule in the name of their absent monarch. Since each Spanish junta claimed authority over Spanish America, the Creoles had to decide which to recognize, and they found it convenient to reject the pretensions of all. Spanish Americans, especially those Creoles who desired independence, proclaimed it their patriotic duty to create similar juntas and to govern themselves until the Desired One returned from his French captivity.

The Caracas aristocrats signed a declaration demanding the right to summon an assembly to rule in the king's name during his absence. Bolívar, who had been meeting secretly with other conspirators on his estate, was not among the signers, for he did not care to follow another's lead. Perhaps his restraint was fortunate on this occasion, for royal officials arrested the author of the declaration. At the same time, however, they kept Bolívar under surveillance.

The arrogance of young Creole aristocrats was well demonstrated by Bolívar in the fall of 1809, when the captain general named him lieutenant chief justice of the Yare valley, where one of Bolívar's estates was located. According to regulations, he took his oath of office before the royal Audiencia, which was composed of judges who were his social equals. Instead of appearing personally before the cabildo, which was composed of men of lower station, he sent his calling card by his solicitor. Offended, the cabildo members refused to receive the solicitor, informing Bolívar that he must report in person to be installed in his office. He protested this affront to the captain general, but what action was taken is unknown. Throughout his life Bolívar would cooperate with others only if he commanded and they obeyed.

In May, 1809, while French armies pushed south in Spain, naval officer Vicente de Emparán arrived in Venezuela as captain general. Because he was an *afrancesado* (pro-French) and had the blessing of Napoleon, he was received with near-hostility by many Venezuelans, but Bolívar and other young conspirators, sensing that he could be useful to them, established close and friendly relations with him. Emparán was accompanied on his arrival by Fernando de Toro, brother of the marqués, as inspector of militia, and by Agustín García, who had been promoted to colonel. Both men were plotters of independence. The Toros had often spoken to Emparán concerning the need for independent action if the French overran all of Spain.

At this time Bolívar, perceiving the royalists' ill-concealed weakness, spoke openly in favor of independence. At a banquet, and in the new captain general's presence, he proposed a toast to the freedom of Venezuela and all of America. Royalist officials, their authority steadily eroding, employed persuasion rather than force to silence him.

The Creole conspirators, convinced that Spain was doomed and would soon be completely occupied by French troops, planned their revolt for April, 1810. The captain general was forewarned, but did nothing more than arrest a few of the leaders and banish Bolívar and others to their country estates, in hope of keeping them apart. When Bolívar and others returned to Caracas a few days later, the captain general took no action against them. Although neither royalists nor Creoles knew it, French troops had already completed the conquest of Spain.

In January a French army had approached Sevilla, and the Junta Central had fled to the Isle of León, connected to the mainland by only a causeway. Disgraced by its military failures, the junta appointed a five-man Regency and disbanded. There was no longer a single governing body representing Ferdinand on Spanish soil, and Joseph seemed to be winning over the people of Andalucía. Royalist officials in Venezuela and other Spanish colonies tried desperately to conceal this news but without success. This was the signal the independence-minded Creoles had awaited, and they went into action almost simultaneously in many Spanish-American cities soon after learning of the French triumph.

In Caracas the cabildo assembled on the night of April 19, and when the captain general arrived, they demanded that he create a representative assembly. Emparán, though invited to preside over the new body, tried to temporize. When he left the meeting to seek the support of royalist sympathizers, the crowd simply escorted him to La Guaira to put him on board a ship to Spain. Bolívar took no part in this affair; according to a cabildo member Bolívar had remained aloof because he was not certain that a government of Creole aristocrats would replace the royal officials.

The independence movement in Caracas, which was still obscured by exclamations of loyalty to Ferdinand the Desired by the more conservative members of the elite, was the work of "radical" Creole aristocrats such as Bolívar. Most of these men, though they might use the language of the eighteenth-century *philosophes,* wanted simply to achieve what they considered their rightful position at the apex of government. They had no intention of encouraging any upward movement of those below them, but they would have to call on these people to do the fighting.

The Creole leaders now decided to send a mission to London, presumably to seek British protection against France. Bolívar, now a colonel of militia, was named to head the delegation when he offered to pay its expenses. Since some of the junta members distrusted his judgment, they named reliable Luis López Méndez to accompany him, and Andrés Bello served as secretary. López Méndez and Bello remained in London, Bello for nearly twenty years. Then, because of the chronic turbulence in his native land, he settled in Chile, where he would play a vital role in Chilean cultural development. The delegates sailed in June, 1810, aboard a British ship.

Britain's position was complicated by the fact that the government was pledged to support Spain against Napoleon, and had acknowledged Ferdinand VII as Spain's rightful monarch. Although the British were tempted by the opportunity to breach Spain's long-standing monopoly of trade with her colonies, they could not, at this time, encourage Spain's colonies to rebel. The Marquis of Wellesley kept Spanish officials informed of the discussions as a subtle means of inspiring the Regency to grant trade concessions. Fearing that the British might treat with the rebels, the Regency authorized trade between Britain and the colonies for the duration of the war with France. Earlier the Regency had authorized the Spanish colonies to trade with European nations, but had withdrawn the decree.

While in England Bolívar was impressed by British power, and realized that Britain could be an invaluable ally. He was also greatly interested in British parliamentary procedures, for he was thinking far ahead to the formation of independent governments in Spanish America. In London, too, he met Miranda. Because of their avowed allegiance to Ferdinand, the Caracas junta members could not negotiate openly with Miranda, but they had instructed Bolívar to listen to his views on the situation in Venezuela, adding discreetly, "and if his present position could in any way that were decent contribute to the aims of the Mission, let him not be rebuffed." In discussing the possibility of Miranda's return to his homeland to assume leadership of the independence movement, Bolívar acted on implied rather than express authority. British officials made mild gestures toward discouraging Miranda from leaving London, but when Bolívar sailed in September on board the British corvette *Sapphire,* he took with him Miranda's papers and baggage. Miranda followed in October on a merchant ship. His return to Venezuela, despite its tragic consequences, was the most significant result of the delegation's efforts in England.

The Spanish Regency, which labored to recover Spain for Ferdinand, was deeply concerned over the possible loss of his empire, and therefore informed the colonies that they were now integral parts of Spain. "From this moment you may consider yourselves raised to the dignity of a free people. You are no longer what you had been, enslaved under a yoke that was the more oppressive because you were so far from the center of power, treated with indifference, pursued by greed and destroyed by ignorance." Spanish Americans were to be represented in the Cortes when that ancient assembly was summoned to meet in Cádiz. But the Regency's generosity, even in time of crisis, was kept under control. Fifteen million Spanish Americans were to send twelve delegates, while the twelve million Spaniards would elect thirty-six. This gesture, intended to conciliate, simply encouraged Creoles to eject royalist officials and to take matters into their own hands. During Bolívar's absence in England the Venezuelan junta had declared freedom of trade with neutral nations, and had abolished both the hated *alcabala,* or sales tax, and the degrading tribute, or head tax, paid by all male Indians.

The Venezuelan Creoles, like those of other Spanish colonies, were divided between desire for independence and innate loyalty to the Spanish monarch. There was also the long-standing antipathy of provincials for the people of the capital, which resulted in many country people siding with the royalists simply because the upper classes of Caracas supported the patriot cause. In the confused struggles that followed, Creoles and *Peninsulares* were found in both patriot and royalist armies, and at first Negroes and *pardos* generally sided with the latter. Royalist power, supported by ships based at Puerto Rico, was strongest in the provinces of Maracaibo, Coro, and Guayana.

When Miranda landed in Venezuela in December, 1810, some Creole aristocrats were not at all delighted to see this sixty-year-old "son of a merchant from the Canaries" who had been away from Venezuela at least forty years, but they needed his military experience, and commissioned him lieutenant general. The Marqués de Toro, whose military knowledge was limited, was commander in chief of the patriot army. Like Bolívar, he owed his military rank to his social standing, not to any demonstrated aptitude for command.

The Venezuelan assembly swore to defend the rights of Ferdinand VII as well as those of the country, but a group of men who wanted an outright declaration of independence created the Patriotic Society and elected Miranda president. Soon this society was accused of destroying national unity by pressuring and undermining the assembly. To these charges Bolívar replied, "What we want is to make unity effective. . . . Let us lay the cornerstone of American freedom without fear. To hesitate is to perish."

Juan Vicente Bolívar, who was disturbed by Miranda's increasing power, was sent as Venezuelan agent to the United States. While there he visited Philadelphia to negotiate an agreement with the Spanish minister, a pact that would guarantee equality between Creoles and *Peninsulares*. This action illustrated once again the conservative Creole aristocrats' attitudes, for Juan Vicente was induced to seek reconciliation with Spain because Miranda was in the ascendant and was trying to "build up a following among the mestizos and mulattoes." Juan Vicente was ordered home, but lost his life in a shipwreck.

As a result of pressure from the Patriotic Society, on April 19, 1811, Venezuela became the first Spanish-American colony to declare independence. Elsewhere patriot leaders, aware that most of their countrymen were blindly loyal to Ferdinand the Desired and the principle of hereditary monarchy, were more discreet, and they disguised their true intentions until the break with Spain could be made without threatening civil war. Venezuela's rash action led immediately to attacks on the government by men professing loyalty to Ferdinand.

In July, as confusion mounted, the congress issued a Declaration of the Rights of the People — liberty, security, property, and equality before the law — but only landowners had the right to vote. In Valencia there was an uprising in which the lower classes, angry that Valencia had not been made a state, supported the royalist cause, and were egged on by *Peninsulares*. On the same day a group of about sixty Canary Islanders, wearing tin helmets and riding mules, cheered Ferdinand and the Virgin Mary and blasted the patriots as traitors. Heading for the arsenal, they were easily defeated and arrested, and nearly a third of them were executed a few days later. Their heads were placed on poles at the city gates to discourage similar royalist demonstrations.

The Marqués de Toro led an expedition against Valencia, but failed to suppress the uprising there. Miranda was asked to command another expedition against Valencia. He agreed, but only on condition that Bolívar would have no part in it.

Miranda's obvious dislike of Bolívar probably resulted from Bolívar's role in representing the Creole aristocracy, for the mutual distrust between Miranda and the aristocrats had not diminished. The two men also disagreed concerning the *Peninsulares*. As the son of a Spaniard, Miranda favored allowing them to remain in the country, while Bolívar proposed to expel them as soon as possible, an action that would have paralyzed the economy. Miranda, who tended toward pomp and theatrics, did not appreciate these qualities in others. Probably, too, each regarded the other as a rival for power.

Although Miranda refused to withdraw his objection, the Marqués de Toro named Bolívar as his own adjutant, enabling Bolívar to take an active part in the fighting against the Valencia rebels. Despite the fact that Miranda was forced back with heavy losses, in his report to the government he named Bolívar along with the other officers cited as deserving praise for their valor. By the time Valencia surrendered, Bolívar had again demonstrated his fighting qualities and gained prestige in the army.

Valencia's capitulation should have been followed immediately by campaigns against Coro and Maracaibo, both royalist strongholds. Bolívar urged prompt attacks on all provinces still under royalist control, but Miranda vacillated while officials in Caracas argued over the wording of the constitution, the form of government, and whether it should be federal or central. The federalists, inspired by the U.S. Constitution, triumphed and created the Federated States of Venezuela under a weak three-man executive committee. Federalism had helped unify the former British colonies, but in Venezuela it proved more a force for disunity than for cohesion. The First Republic was from its creation doomed by fatal flaws. At a critical time, when the firmest unity was demanded, the country was becoming increasingly chaotic and disunited. The choice of Valencia as the seat of the government offended other cities. The economy was in ruins and the government, unable to find adequate sources of income, turned to the universal panacea of amateur politicians — paper, ink, and a printing press. The flood of paper money caused rapid inflation, and discontent intensified. New obstacles arose daily, and the government's mild policy was inappropriate for the deadly struggle. The government planned expeditions against royalist strongholds, but these were frustrated by an unexpected and unavoidable calamity.

On March 26, 1812 (Holy Thursday), Caracas and other cities received signs of what many considered divine wrath. That afternoon was suffocatingly hot and ominously quiet. Rain fell briefly though no clouds were in sight. Then the earth writhed violently, and houses and other buildings crumbled and fell. Cries of trapped and injured people were heard on every side, while priests and monks walked among the ruins loudly damning the godless traitors who had been disloyal to their king. Frightened and repentant people fell on their knees, wailing "Mercy! King Ferdinand!"

Bolívar rushed into the rubble-littered streets to help the injured. To the archbishop, he declared, "If nature opposes us, we shall fight against her and force her to obey."

Because the towns held by the patriots were the hardest hit — in Caracas the death toll was at least 10,000 — the independence movement was held responsible for the catastrophe that struck the First Republic a deadly blow. Royalist priests made the most of the opportunity and scared the masses witless by their tirades from pulpit and street corner. Since both the revolution and the earthquake had occurred on a Holy Thursday, the coincidence was cited as proof that Divine Providence had chosen that date to demonstrate anger at the rebels. The government's flood of proclamations assuring the people that earthquakes were natural phenomena made no headway in checking the contagious religious hysteria.

The governor of Maracaibo, sensing an opportunity to give the First Republic its deathblow, had organized a force of 500 men and sent them, under royalist naval captain Domingo Monteverde, against the federal capital at Valencia. Royalist uprisings had erupted in many places, while the inexperienced congressmen debated the constitutionality of ordering the patriot army to march against Monteverde. Patriot troops, especially cavalry units, deserted en masse to join the royalists, and an influential Indian, Juan de los Reyes Vargas, was persuaded by a priest to forsake the patriots and follow Monteverde.

In desperation the patriot congress named Miranda commander in chief, granting him virtually dictatorial powers to meet the crisis. Many young men such as Bolívar were eager to fight for their country, but Miranda sent Bolívar to defend Puerto Cabello, the most important harbor in patriot control. Despite the vital need to hold Puerto Cabello, Bolívar, who had requested active service, regarded his assignment as a subtle device for keeping him from sharing in the fighting and the glory that went with victory. "Fame consists of being great and useful," he said later, and he saw no opportunity for fame, despite the fact that Puerto Cabello was clearly a royalist target. Although he should have been much concerned over the multitude of royalist prisoners in the fortress of San Felipe under his command, he seems to have left too much to his subordinates and, like Achilles, sulked in his tent.

Monteverde, who allowed his troops to loot every town they occupied, entered Valencia virtually without opposition. Surprised at the ease of the conquest, he determined to hold the city, and called for reinforcements. Miranda, as if in a trance, took no decisive action, allowing the royalist reinforcements to enter Valencia unopposed.

Royalist uprisings continued to spread, encouraged by Miranda's inaction, and in some towns patriot soldiers were mutilated and whole populations annihilated. As the royalists closed in around Caracas, the patriots became desperate, but Miranda supinely burned his precious military stores and abandoned a position that a few determined men could have held. On his retreat to La Victoria, his rear guard routed Monteverde's advance troops. A swift pursuit of the royalists could have saved the patriot cause, but though his officers begged him to act quickly and take advantage of the opportunity, Miranda seemed to shun any offensive action.

Royalist successes and conspirators won over Lieutenant

Francisco Vinoni and some of Bolívar's troops, who raised the royalist flag over the fort of San Felipe and released the royalist prisoners. With few men still loyal and most of his ammunition in the hands of the enemy, Bolívar was in a perilous position. His offer of amnesty to the deserters was ignored. He sent a message to Miranda that unless he attacked the enemy from the rear, Puerto Cabello was lost. "Meanwhile," he concluded, "I shall hold out as long as I can." Eight years later he gained a measure of revenge when his troops captured Vinoni after a patriot victory. Bolívar ordered him summarily hanged for treason.

Miranda made no move to help Bolívar, whose troops, outnumbered ten to one, held on desperately for six days through a heavy bombardment that killed 120 of them. When Miranda received Bolívar's message that San Felipe had been lost, he said only, "That is the way of the world. A little while ago we thought all was secure. Yesterday Monteverde had neither weapons nor ammunition. To-day he has both in abundance. I am told to attack the enemy. But he already has everything in his hands. To-morrow we shall see what happens."

Many patriot officers, including Bolívar, had already concluded that Miranda was an ineffective commander and a liability to the cause. An aggressive fighting man was needed, not a passive philosopher. Miranda's tragedy was that the independence movement began too late in his life for him to take an active part in it. His contribution had been to promote the idea of independence among scores of future Spanish-American leaders. When it was time for him to remain on the sidelines as a spectator, he was thrown into the midst of a deadly conflict, a bewildered misfit who brought only destruction and sorrow to the people he would free.

Bolívar never forgot his first defeat, for he was aware that he had been unwise in holding prisoners in the same fortress where his munitions were stored. And a conspiracy had been hatched among his men without his knowledge or suspicion of it, even though he knew that there were wealthy royalists among the prisoners and that patriot troops were inexperienced and unreliable. In a moment of deep chagrin he wrote Miranda that he felt incapable of command, though self-doubts were most uncharacteristic of him.

The loss of Puerto Cabello, though critical, was not necessarily fatal for the patriots, for prompt and aggressive action might yet have saved them. But Miranda simply watched while disgusted patriot troops went over to the royalists. Apparently he was convinced that Venezuelans were not ready for independence. Unknown to his officers, he sent an agent to negotiate an armistice with Monteverde, then, doubting Monteverde's sincerity, went to La Guaira to secure passage on a ship. Under the terms of the agreement only the people of the provinces as yet unconquered by royalists were to escape persecution and confiscation of property.

After reporting to the Caracas cabildo on the armistice with Monteverde, Miranda sent his papers and some treasure to La Guaira to be loaded on the *Sapphire,* which made a timely arrival. When Miranda reached La Guaira the captain urged him to board at once, but he insisted on remaining ashore for the night. He had not informed anyone of the terms of the capitulation, and by the time Bolívar and other officers learned of it Monteverde's troops were already at the gates of Caracas. All of the patriot officers were outraged at Miranda's actions, regarding him as the betrayer of his countrymen. When in La Guaira they demanded an explanation, Miranda was more rude than informative.

A rumor spread that Miranda had given orders that none of the officers was to be allowed to leave Venezuela, convincing Bolívar and his companions that Miranda had indeed betrayed the cause of independence and sacrificed his countrymen, who were determined to continue the struggle. The officers met that night to decide a course of action. Bolívar and others argued that Miranda should be shot for treason, while some suggested merely that he be prevented from leaving the country. Before dawn they awakened Miranda and arrested him, taking him to the fortress of San Carlos for incarceration. Their intention was to force him to remain in the country so that he could insist on Monteverde's fulfilling the terms of the capitulation.

That same day Monteverde ordered the port closed, adding that if this were not done all previous concessions were nullified. The commander of San Carlos hauled down the patriot flag and raised Spanish colors, which made Miranda a royalist prisoner. He was eventually imprisoned in Cádiz, where he died in 1816, all but forgotten by Creole and royalist alike.

The treatment of Miranda has been much discussed by Bolívar's contemporaries as well as by his and Miranda's biographers. Francisco José Heredia, a Creole born in Santo Domingo who had been appointed judge of the Audiencia of Caracas in 1809, was one of the harshest critics at the time. "While in La Guaira," he wrote with regard to Bolívar, "when Miranda went there to embark, he was one of those who plotted and carried out the arrest of this unfortunate man, his intimate friend, whom he had previously taken pride in having brought to Venezuela; an infamous act, from the black stain of which he will never be able to wash his reputation." Bolívar remained convinced that he had acted properly, and never expressed any regret over Miranda's fate.

Monteverde quickly demonstrated that the surrender terms meant nothing, for he began widespread persecution of all suspected of having fought for independence. He sent eight civilian leaders — "eight monsters," he called them — in chains to Cádiz, in violation of the capitulation. Because he was certain that his actions would be unacceptable to the Regency, Monteverde claimed that they had committed treasonable acts after the surrender. The Regency repeatedly demanded that he produce proof of his allegations, but although he did not comply, the Regency did not release either these prisoners or Miranda.

Bolívar returned to Caracas in disguise and hid in the house of the Marqués de Casas León. Later he asked Francisco Iturbe, a Basque friend who knew Monteverde well, to secure a pass for him so that he could leave Venezuela. Monteverde hesitated, for he knew that Bolívar was an ardent patriot. Iturbe offered himself as a guarantee for Bolívar's conduct, and when Monteverde's resistance seemed nearly overcome he brought Bolívar to him. "Here is the commander of Puerto Cabello for whom I have offered my bond. . . . My life stands for his."

"Very well," Monteverde replied. Turning to his secretary, he said, "This gentleman is to be issued a pass as a reward for the service he rendered the king by the arrest of Miranda."

Having more pride than discretion, Bolívar corrected him. "I had Miranda arrested to punish him for betraying his country," he said, "not to serve the king." Monteverde stopped his secretary from writing the pass, but when Iturbe redoubled his pleas, finally relented. Bolívar would later have an opportunity to repay Iturbe, but for the next few years Monteverde blanched whenever he heard Bolívar's name.

At La Guaira Bolívar boarded the first ship to sail, but since its papers were not in proper order the Dutch customs officer at Curaçao seized Bolívar's baggage. As a result he remained there several months, while deciding on his next move. With him were other patriot officers from Venezuela.

Bolívar was about five feet, six inches in height, with broad chest, slender body, and the small hands and feet of the aristocrat. He had a high forehead, black hair, high cheekbones, and a sensual — some said ugly — mouth. His facial expressions changed as rapidly as his moods. He disliked being alone, and was almost never without women companions, even on campaign.

To understand Bolívar's tenacity it is necessary to consider the Spanish-American cult of *machismo*, part of the legacy of the conquistadores. The *macho* is, or believes himself to be, the kind of man women pursue and men follow willingly, a combination of Casanova, torero, and gaucho. The typical macho makes a constant display of his manliness — in its pure state machismo reflects courage, honor, and dignity, but too often it is mere braggadocio. Would-be machos boast of their endless boudoir triumphs yet assert that they marry only virgins and defend their sisters' honor to the death, but the contradictory nature of these claims raises doubts among both skeptics and statisticians. The fundamental characteristic of machismo is power. Bolívar was a true macho, and it was this quality that made it impossible for him to serve under another or to admit defeat, and so was a vital factor in his perseverance in the discouraging struggle for independence.

Bolívar was at this time thirty years old, and learning with every experience. The First Venezuelan Republic had survived only one year, but he was not discouraged by the Herculean task ahead; at this stage of his career he had only one major goal — to break all ties that bound Venezuela to the Spanish Empire. He and his companions sailed for Cartagena, a fortified port city in New Granada, to resume the fight for Venezuelan independence.

TWO

The Second Republic

In 1812 the Spanish Cortes met at Cádiz to write a constitution for Spain. The Spanish colonies had been invited to send deputies; since for various reasons not all were able to get to Cádiz, Creoles residing in Spain provided alternate representation. Bolívar's uncle Esteban Palacios, and Fermín Clemente, both living in Spain at the time, represented Venezuela. The Junta Central had neglected to summon delegates from the *grandes* (nobility), archbishops, and bishops, so the majority of the delegates were of liberal persuasion, and they drew up a constitution to their liking. It was not exactly Spain's first constitution, for Napoleon had called an assembly of Spanish notables to Bayonne, where he gave them the guidelines for the so-called Bayonne Constitution of 1808. It was a reasonably good document but Spaniards resented its source, and it was in effect only in areas held by the French army.

Many Spaniards and Spanish Americans hoped that the new Constitution of 1812 would undermine the colonial independence movement. Bolívar had no such delusions, and his determination to liberate Venezuela was in no way diminished. In mid-November, 1812, after abandoning his property held by the customs office in Curaçao, he and his companions arrived at Cartagena to resume the struggle. They found Bolívar's uncle José Félix Ribas and many other Venezuelans already there.

In New Granada the patriots were still largely in control but so badly divided that the period has been labeled the *patria bobo,* or foolish fatherland. Patriots controlled the interior, but a bitter struggle between federalist and centralist factions was under way. Some coastal provinces had not declared for independence, and remained resolutely royalist. A few cities favored independence but refused to acknowledge Bogotá's authority over them — Cartagena was one of these. Under young Manuel Rodríguez Torices it had established an independent government. Rodríguez Torices was well aware that he needed an army to prevent a royalist reconquest, and he welcomed Bolívar and those with him into the army of Cartagena.

In the months since Venezuela's shocking collapse Bolívar had reflected much on the independence movement, and he expressed his thoughts in an appeal to the people of New Granada. Pointing out that the catastrophe in Venezuela should serve as an object lesson to all Americans, he emphasized the need for unity, solidarity, and energetic government. The acceptance of a federal constitution had broken social contracts and encouraged anarchy; this, he believed, was the basic cause of the First Republic's downfall. Each province had been virtually independent. What was needed, he stated forcefully, was strong centralized government.

"Our compatriots" he wrote, "are not yet capable of exercising their legal rights." They lacked the virtues of true republicans. "Moreover," he added, "what country on earth can afford a weak and intricate system of government such as a federation of states, where different factions quarrel within and war threatens from without?" Bolívar the statesman was emerging. He was still the revolutionary, but he had become an advocate of a strong, centralized, authoritarian government in order to win the war.

Government must accommodate itself to circumstances, he advised the Granadinos, and then it will be firm and effective. But if the circumstances are confused and perilous, the government must be "formidable and ruthless," disregarding laws and constitutions. Until they united, their enemies would have all the advantages. Civil war would prevail, and they would be "shamefully beaten by that little horde of bandits — which pollutes our country." The cause of Venezuela's misfortunes was not the royalists, but disunity that led them back into slavery. "A strong government could have changed everything. It would even have been able to master the moral confusion which ensued after the earthquake. With it, Venezuela would today be free."

Bolívar pointed out that, for its own safety, New Granada needed to liberate Venezuela, which required the conquest of Caracas. The only solution was to take the offensive. "Under no circumstances," he warned, "must we remain on the defensive." Bolívar's "Manifesto de Cartagena" won him widespread support in New Granada. "Is there," he asked, "an American worthy of the name, who would not cry 'Death to all Spaniards!' when he beheld the destruction of so many victims in Venezuela? No, and No again!" These words marked the beginning of Bolívar's effective political pronouncements and his role as spiritual leader of the independence movement in the north.

By this time Bolívar was thinking of northern South America, not simply Venezuela, for he realized that disunity was a general characteristic of Spanish Americans. He was also thinking beyond independence, for he already envisioned a confederated government of all Spanish-American states from Venezuela to Upper Peru (modern Bolivia). His ideas were premature, and that they would prove chimerical was only one of his tragedies.

Bolívar's message was most appropriate for the people of New Granada, who had created a supreme council in July, 1810. After that the rifts between factions had led to the *patria bobo*. The province of Cundinamarca had raised its own congress in opposition to that of Bogotá; the Federation of New Granadan Provinces arose, with its capital at Tunja. Antonio Nariño headed the government at Bogotá; Camilo Torres was the federalist leader at Tunja. Both were genuine patriots, admirable men devoted to their country's welfare, but their political differences and their refusal to compromise proved calamitous. As a result of this situation, Bolívar had to appeal not only to the government of Cartagena but to those of Bogotá and Tunja as well to help liberate Venezuela. If he had not inspired complete confidence in all three governments, his would have been an empty dream.

The royalists still held the lower Magdalena region as well as the valleys along the border between New Granada and Venezuela. Royalist posts on the Magdalena River cut Cartagena's communications with Bogotá, leaving the city exposed on both flanks. French captain Pierre Labatut, who had served in Venezuela, commanded the army of Cartagena. He ordered Bolívar to defend Barrancas, a village on the left bank of the Magdalena, instructing him not to initiate any action unless he received orders.

Bolívar's military training and experience had been limited, and the upcoming campaigns provided his basic military education, although he continued to learn the ways of war on the battlefield. There was much to be learned, but he was a diligent student. He organized a small but effective force of 200 men. Knowing the patriot cause was jeopardized by royalist control of the lower Magdalena, he ignored his instructions and immediately set out upstream, transporting his troops on rafts. At Tenerife the royalist garrison rejected his demand to surrender but fled when his troops attacked, leaving much-needed ships and munitions. Bolívar and his men pushed on upriver to Mompox, where many young Granadinos joined the patriot force. As Bolívar commented later, "I was born in Caracas, but my fame was born in Mompox." After two furiously active weeks he could write the Congress of New Granada that he had cleared the Magdalena of royalists as far as Ocaña, where he established his headquarters while waiting for permission to march toward Venezuela. His superior, Labatut, angrily demanded that Bolívar be court-martialed for insubordination, but Rodríguez Torices defended him.

In the meantime a thousand royalist troops from Venezuela occupied the border town of Cúcuta and threatened the Granadino army of Colonel Manuel del Castillo, commander of the province of Pamplona. Supported by both Camilo Torres and Antonio Nariño, Bolívar marched on Cúcuta with 400 men, a journey that took him from the tropical lowlands across cold and bleak mountain passes. Because men accustomed to the tropical lowlands suffered intensely from extreme cold, Bolívar had to march among them and inspire them to make them look ahead to future glory and forget present discomforts. He succeeded, and reached Cúcuta late in February, when he immediately launched an attack. His men soon exhausted their ammunition, but they charged with fixed bayonets while the royalists abandoned their positions and dashed toward

Venezuela. The outstanding victory at Cúcuta greatly strengthened Bolívar's small army, for the money and munitions captured from the enemy were badly needed. Equally important were the lessons Bolívar learned concerning the handling of troops on difficult marches, and getting them into battle in a mood to conquer. New Granada was temporarily freed from danger of a royalist invasion from that quarter. Camilo Torres promoted Bolívar to brigadier general in the army of the confederacy and gave him permission to make a diversionary thrust into Venezuela.

While Bolívar was preparing to fight his way into Venezuela from the west, other patriot forces had invaded eastern Venezuela. When Monteverde entered Caracas the previous year, the eastern provinces had capitulated. He sent Francisco Cervériz there as military commander, and an indiscriminate slaughter of Creoles began. "Not one who falls into my hands shall escape," he boasted to Monteverde. He followed the old maxim that "four walls for a prison are three too many" — he needed only one wall and a firing squad.

A small group of patriots — including young Santiago Mariño, bold and uncontrollable Francisco Bermúdez, and Manuel Piar, an ambitious and violent mulatto from Curaçao — evaded the royalists and fled to Chacachacare, an island near Trinidad. As royalist persecutions spread, other patriots joined them.

With fewer than fifty men and only a few guns, Mariño led the first patriot landing on the coast of Venezuela in January, 1813, while Bolívar was in New Granada clearing the lower Magdalena of royalists. Mariño's men routed a small royalist force in the port of Paria, capturing weapons and recruiting natives. Mariño's continued successes enabled him to amass and arm a respectable fighting force, with which he harassed royalists in the eastern provinces.

Fearful of losing the entire province of Cumaná, Monteverde sent 500 men under the Basque Antonio Zuazola, one of the most brutal of royalist officers. Well aware of Zuazola's atrocities, the entrenched patriots fought furiously, preferring death in battle to surrender. Monteverde also attacked Mariño's army at Maturín, but lost fifteen officers, most of his men, all of his equipment, and barely escaped capture himself.

Bolívar divided his army into two divisions under Colonel Manuel del Castillo and José Félix Ribas for the march to Mérida and Trujillo. On the way Bolívar determined to slice through royalist lines and dash for Caracas. At this time patriot colonel Nicolás Briceño, a subordinate of Castillo, proclaimed war to the death against all Spaniards and Canary Islanders, and the campaign became excessively brutal. Although Briceño's main purpose was collecting loot from wealthy royalists, his declared objective was to terrorize the enemy into leaving the country. One town he entered contained only two *Peninsulares,* both in their eighties. When Briceño sent their heads to Bolívar and Castillo, each grisly trophy accompanied by a letter written partly in the victim's blood, both men were shocked. Castillo ordered Briceño to refrain from punishments without respecting legal forms. Bolívar also protested. "Henceforth," he ordered, "you shall on no account shoot or carry out any other major sentence without first putting before me the proceedings . . . in accordance with the laws and orders of the government. . . ."

Jealousies among patriot officers created other problems that often jeopardized the goals, and Bolívar now found Colonel Castillo opposing him. His offer to serve under Castillo was spurned, but when Bolívar submitted his resignation the government named him commander of all troops in the north, again making him Castillo's senior. He ordered Castillo to attack the royalists in La

Grita; Castillo procrastinated, then defeated the enemy force on April 13. Following his victory he left his advance troops in La Grita, returned to Cúcuta, and resigned, saying that invading Venezuela with New Granada's troops offended his "moral principles." He was replaced by a young Granadino officer, Francisco de Paula Santander, who later played a prominent role in the independence wars and after, first as Bolívar's friend, then as his enemy. It was a critical period for Bolívar, for the only real authority or influence he had over Granadino troops was what his personality achieved.

When Bolívar ordered Santander to march, at first he also refused. Knowing that rebellion would spread quickly among the New Granada troops and that all would be lost, Bolívar quickly faced Santander. "March!" he ordered. "Either you shoot me or, by God, I'll shoot you!" Santander marched, and remained obedient to Bolívar thereafter. By such bold and theatrical actions Bolívar finally won control of his army, and he crossed into Venezuela in May, eight months after fleeing from his native land. The rift between New Granada and Venezuela reflected in Castillo's actions remained, never to heal. Colonel Rafael Urdaneta sent Bolívar words of encouragement. "General," he wrote, "if two men are enough to free the country, I am ready to go with you."

Royalist commander Colonel Ramón Correa, seeing the whole population of the Mérida-Trujillo area bitterly antiroyalist owing to brutal treatment by his predecessors, withdrew after Castillo defeated him at La Grita. A *Peninsular*, Vicente Campo Elías, immediately led a movement to proclaim independence — not merely independence from Spain, but total elimination of all *Peninsulares*. "I should destroy all Spaniards," he exclaimed, "and then shoot myself so that not a single man remain of this accursed race."

When the bloodthirsty royalist commander Zuazola was captured by patriots, Bolívar offered to exchange him for Colonel Diego Jalón, a Spanish-born patriot held by Monteverde. Probably happy to be rid of his murderous Basque subordinate, Monteverde refused, but declared that he was willing to exchange officers of "equal character." He added that he would kill two Creoles for every *Peninsular* killed by the patriots. Bolívar met bombast with bombast: "If the intruding ex-Governor Monteverde is ready to sacrifice two Americans for every Spaniard or Canarian, the Liberator of Venezuela is ready to sacrifice 6,000 Spaniards or Canarians he holds in his power for the first American victim." He ordered Zuazola hanged; Monteverde spared Jalón, but had four other patriot officers shot.

A short time later Bolívar heard that Briceño and others had been captured near Barinas by royalists, who shot all of them as rebels. Angered by this and other examples of royalist brutality, on June 8 Bolívar issued a proclamation.

> Those executioners who call themselves our enemies have broken international law. . . . But the victims will be avenged, these executioners exterminated. Our vengeance shall equal the cruelties of the Spaniards, for our forbearance is exhausted. Since our oppressors forced us into this deadly war, they will vanish from the face of America. . . . Our hatred knows no bounds, and the war shall be to the death!

Bolívar followed this with another proclamation, pardoning all natives for past acts against the patriots, but sparing the lives of only those *Peninsulares* who would actively and effectively support the patriots. "Spaniards and Canary Islanders," the proclamation concluded, "be prepared for certain death, even if you are merely indif-

ferent. Americans, you shall live, even if you are guilty."
Briceño was shot as expected and as he undoubtedly deserved, but others captured with him were not.

The War to the Death now began. There has been
much speculation concerning Bolívar's motives for proclaiming it. Avenging royalist atrocities against innocent
people was certainly one reason, but not the major one.
Rafael Urdaneta, Bolívar's chief of staff who suggested the
idea to him, explained: "From this two necessary consequences flowed — the Spaniards, knowing they would find
certain death, would be cowed, as actually happened; the
Creoles would flock back to Bolívar's arms, as it was necessary they should. The result, the occupation of Caracas,
fully justified the measure." Bolívar later commented that
"to bind to us four guerrillas, who contributed to our liberation, it was necessary to declare the War to the Death."
Most likely, Bolívar saw in it a sure means of ending the
neutrality or indifference of many Venezuelans and of
making reconciliation with Spain impossible, even under
the liberal Constitution of 1812. The main effect of the
War to the Death was to make Venezuela a desert.

Bolívar's drive for Caracas was jeopardized by the royalist reconquest of Santa Marta and threat to Cartagena, for
the congress ordered him to stay in Mérida. If he obeyed,
Bolívar knew, Monteverde would assemble a superior
force and destroy his own small army. "More than ever,"
he wrote to the congress, "we must act with speed and
force. If we remain passive, or take one step backward, all
will be lost. . . ." He had decided, therefore, to strike the
royalists in Barinas, which would leave New Granada free
from enemies in that direction.

In this guerrilla-like action Bolívar faced danger from
royalist forces in Maracaibo and Coro as well as Barinas,
where royalists under Antonio Tizcar were trying to block
his escape route. Bolívar crossed the cordillera and, with

information gained from the propatriot population, surprised and defeated the enemy. Immediately after the victory he enlisted 400 royalist prisoners in the patriot army. In little more than a month the swift movements of patriot forces under Bolívar and José Félix Ribas had cleared the Mérida-Trujillo-Barinas region of royalists. In Barinas Bolívar acquired a supply of arms and ammunition as well as 200,000 pesos to pay his troops.

About the time Bolívar entered Barinas, Monteverde was on his way to Valencia, where he allowed every Basque and Canary Islander to select an enemy to be imprisoned. When Bolívar and Ribas met in San Carlos, their force had grown to 2,500 men; only 1,200 royalists blocked the road to Caracas. As the enemy withdrew toward Valencia, Bolívar ordered that both a cavalryman and an infantryman mount each of the 200 strongest horses, and sent them dashing to cut off the enemy retreat, while he followed with the rest of his troops. The maneuver was successful, and the battle of Taguanos that followed was Bolívar's first major victory. When he learned of the royalist defeat, Monteverde abandoned Valencia to the patriots and withdrew to Puerto Cabello.

On entering Valencia Bolívar was confronted by Basques and Canary Islanders who had supported Monteverde. Despite the pleas of many people, he ordered all of them shot the same day. His rapid moves and the use of terror had opened the way to Caracas. When La Victoria surrendered, Bolívar announced that "this capitulation shall be religiously respected, to the shame of the perfidious Monteverde and to the glory of the American name." The terror had already served its purpose.

In La Victoria Bolívar received a delegation sent from the Caracas junta to negotiate with him, a delegation which included his friends Iturbe and the Marqués de Casas León. Because of the War to the Death many families had already fled Caracas, and others were apprehensive. Bolívar received the delegation warmly, but while assuring them of amnesty, he demanded that the city of La Guaira also surrender.

On August 6, 1813, two weeks after his thirtieth birthday, Bolívar entered Caracas in triumph, welcomed by twelve white-robed maidens who placed a laurel crown on his head. It was the kind of ceremony that delighted Bolívar, and one of the maidens, Josefina Madrid, soon shared his couch. Known as "Señorita Pepa," she gloried in the power her new position gave her, and proved herself as vindictive as she was adept at intrigue.

Bolívar having entered Valencia, the royalists were restricted to Puerto Cabello, Maracaibo, and Coro. Monteverde held Puerto Cabello, which Bolívar should have reduced before advancing to Caracas. He sent a force to lay siege to the city and fortress, explaining that he had gone straight to Caracas because the city's population was torn between royalists and patriots. Earlier, however, in a letter to Camilo Torres he had noted the successes of the patriot army in the east under Mariño, and his defeat of Monteverde at Maturín. He was fearful that Mariño would enter Caracas at any moment. "But we shall fly, and I hope no liberator will tread the ruins of Caracas before me." His haste to enter Caracas was for fame and glory, but if he had lacked such powerful motives he might well have abandoned the cause of independence long before the exhausting struggle was over.

Before launching a campaign to destroy the remaining royalist forces Bolívar established a government, ordering Francisco Javier de Ustariz to draw up a plan for a constitution. This was no simple assignment, for there were certain basic problems to be resolved — the desire for local autonomy, called "federalism"; the wish of some for a weak republican government exclusive of the army; the custom of the upper classes to ignore any government that interfered with them; and the innate loyalty of the masses to the king. Ustariz suggested that the executive and legislative powers be conferred on the commander in chief of the army, who would guide government officials in the formulation of policies. As a result, Bolívar assumed the role of dictator, and named three trusted men to head the departments of state, war, and justice. As long as the war continued, authoritarian rule was necessary, for the patriot cause would have disintegrated otherwise. Only Bolívar's political opponents criticized him for refusing to reestablish the weak federal government Monteverde had easily overthrown in 1812.

In order to gain a measure of control over the lower classes, the cooperation of the Church was needed, for the archbishop had urged Venezuelans to acknowledge only the government of Ferdinand. Bolívar demanded a retraction, without success, then began courting the lower clergy, for many of the parish priests sympathized with the patriot cause.

Bolívar also encouraged *Peninsulares* to emigrate, hoping to replace them and Creoles lost in the War to the Death with immigrants. To stimulate the royalists' desire to leave Venezuela, he warned Monteverde that unless he surrendered Puerto Cabello every royalist in Caracas would be shot. Monteverde refused, but Bolívar did not immediately carry out his threat.

Venezuela, badly torn by the destructive warfare, was in severe financial straits, and smuggling deprived the government of customs duties. To support his army Bolívar decreed that each property owner, shopkeeper, and priest contribute to the government the cost of maintaining at least one soldier. Since funds accumulated slowly, he decided on forced donations. "Nothing but utter impossibility will be deemed a valid excuse," he instructed his subordinates, "and by shooting three or four of those who may refuse, you will teach obedience to others." Building up and training an army out of unpromising human elements was his major accomplishment during the early months of his administration — a task that required charisma more than military prowess. At the same time he slashed government expenditures, saying that there was "no lack of good men who are satisfied with the bare necessities of life." He would employ them, he said, in all branches of the administration.

Recruitment of the lower classes was difficult in a war fought for the benefit of the upper classes. As Bolívar once admitted, we have "democracy on our lips, aristocracy in our hearts." His political sense made him see that the war could not be won without the *pardos,* for in some places Negroes and mulattoes declared in favor of Ferdinand. Bolívar became a thorough advocate of legal equality for all. When volunteers were called for, Colonel José Félix Ribas, military governor of Caracas, issued a proclamation reflecting his disappointment in the lack of response.

> The Government has seen with utter amazement that the call to arms sounded this morning had no effect whatever. . . . The call to arms shall be repeated this afternoon, at four, and anyone not present in the Main Plaza or not in the Capuchin Canton, or found at home or in the street, shall be shot with no more than three hours of chapel, and no other justification than that needed to prove his absence.

General Juan Manuel de Cagigal, royalist commander in Barcelona (and later successor to Monteverde when he suffered a serious wound), was much discouraged by Mariño's successes. Leaving 100 men with orders to begin guerrilla warfare, he withdrew to Guayana. Mariño, considering himself equal or superior to Bolívar, entered Barcelona and declared himself Dictator of the East.

Knowing that the war was by no means ended, Bolívar made overtures to Mariño, suggesting that they cooperate against the royalists. "Divided, we will be weaker," Bolívar wrote him, but Mariño enjoyed his newfound power and refused to accept any of Bolívar's proposals. He was both young and easily flattered, and Piar and other subordinates encouraged his independent attitude, although in the long run it could benefit only the royalists.

There was also the problem of the *Peninsular* and Creole royalist supporters who remained in the country, for they were conspiring against the patriot regime. Bolívar organized an effective spy system, and on the basis of information it gathered, scotched one supposed conspiracy by executing more than sixty Creole and *Peninsular* royalists without trial.

The need to take Puerto Cabello was still urgent, for the patriot siege force could not prevent the royalists from receiving supplies and reinforcements by sea. Early in September Bolívar learned that a Spanish naval squadron was bringing seasoned veterans of the Napoleonic wars to reinforce Monteverde. The arrival of 1,200 fresh troops and ample munitions enabled Monteverde to force Bolívar to lift the siege. In the fighting Monteverde was wounded, but Bolívar suffered a greater loss when Atanasio Girardot, a New Granada officer, one of the ablest in the patriot army, was killed. The royalists quickly cut the lines of communication between Venezuela and New Granada.

European affairs affected the independence struggles, for in December, 1813, Napoleon made peace with Spain, acknowledged Ferdinand as king, and agreed to withdraw French troops from the Peninsula. A month later Joseph abdicated, a mere formality, for he was already among the ranks of unemployed monarchs. In March, 1814, Ferdinand the Desired returned to Spain. This was what many Spanish Americans had believed they were fighting for, and the independence movements everywhere moved toward the nadir.

Once back in power in Madrid, however, Ferdinand gradually rekindled the desire for freedom throughout the Spanish colonies, until it was stronger than before. He immediately disavowed the Constitution of 1812 and declared void all acts of the Cortes, decreeing further that anyone who advocated obedience to either was guilty of *lese majesté*, a crime punishable by death. All of the important liberals in or out of the Cortes were persecuted, including Spanish-American deputies. Some liberals were ordered executed by royal decree, for the judges could find no crimes that had been committed.

The Inquisition, which the Cortes had abolished in 1813, was restored, and royal absolutism was revived. The years from 1814 to 1820 were years of reaction and terror in Spain. Many men in both Spain and Spanish America who had risked their lives to preserve Ferdinand's crown and empire were driven into the opposition. Ferdinand's senseless and brutal despotism ultimately saved the cause of Spanish-American independence.

Campo Elías cleared the Calabozo regime of royalists, but his reprisals for royalist atrocities did not increase the patriots' popularity on the llanos. Urdaneta, campaigning in the Barquisimeto area meanwhile, was checked by a larger royalist force under Colonel José Ceballos. Bolívar joined him with reinforcements and attacked Ceballos on November 10, but was forced to fall back. With fresh reinforcements they drove the royalists off. Colonel José Yáñez joined Ceballos while Campo Elías united forces with Bolívar and Urdaneta. On December 5, 1813, they met the royalists on the plains between San Carlos and Guanare. The battle was going in favor of the royalists when Bolívar, at the head of a select cavalry squadron, charged the enemy cavalry and turned the tide in favor of the patriots. The victory was one of the most significant for the patriots in the war up to that time, for they inflicted heavy losses on the royalists and quickly mustered the captured Venezuelan royalists into the patriot ranks.

After the victory, which was a milestone in Bolívar's military education, he issued a proclamation in which he offered to pardon all Venezuelans who came to any of the patriot headquarters within a month. To his sorrow the offer was largely ignored, and Venezuelans continued to enlist in the royalist army. Some of the most stubborn and fanatic royalists throughout the wars were not Spaniards but Venezuelans and Granadinos.

In Venezuela the royalist cause revived in 1814 with a surge of llaneros, or plainsmen, under José Tomás Boves, a Spaniard interested in loot who had traded for horses and mules on the vast llanos. Among the llaneros he had earned a reputation for brute strength and fair dealing. After rough treatment by a band of patriot troops, he became an ardent enemy of the patriots rather than an enthusiastic supporter of the royalists. In the fall of 1813 he and Francisco Morales, a Canary Islander, mobilized the llaneros for the royalist cause. Both men were bold and ruthless, and the hundreds of mulatto, mestizo, and Negro llaneros they recruited were fearless fighters and excellent horsemen, adept with the lance. This "Legion of Hell," under its sadistic leaders, gave the War to the Death a real meaning, for they spared no one. The speed of their movements was astonishing, and the devastation they caused left populous areas empty wastelands. Under Boves and Morales an even more brutal phase of the war began. As Daniel Florencio O'Leary commented, "Of all the monsters produced by revolution in America or elsewhere,

José Tomás Boves was the most bloodthirsty and ferocious."

The patriots had little choice but to meet terror with terror, and anyone who fell into the hands of either side was shot. The war became more fanatic and destructive than ever, a death-struggle between city and country, between the haves and the have-nots. As military commander of Calabozo, Boves was so tyrannical that the people persuaded Monteverde to send him to serve under General Cagigal in the campaign against Mariño. Soon after this Cagigal withdrew and left Boves and Morales free to do as they wished.

In January, 1814, Bolívar resigned his authority, but despite his warning that a victorious soldier had not earned the right to rule his country, the Venezuelan government granted him dictatorial powers. He accepted these powers, but only until the danger was past. For the patriots 1814 was a year of frantic troop movements and costly battles, for there were not enough troops to defend all fronts at once. Both Boves and Yáñez made strikes toward Caracas. On one occasion Campo Elías defeated Boves near Calabozo and decimated his force, taking no prisoners. Following this action the patriot army shot about one-fourth of the people of Calabozo for not having taken up arms against Boves. Brutality bred brutality, and once the War to the Death began in earnest, a number of patriot officers proved quite as merciless as the llanero chieftains.

Knowing that with Mariño's cooperation the patriots could defeat the llaneros, Bolívar continued his friendly overtures toward him. Mariño remained unmoved, although lack of unity invited disaster in the face of growing royalist strength on the coast and the llanos. Boves defeated the patriots at La Puerta and advanced on Caracas. In desperation Bolívar pleaded with Mariño to attack Boves's army from the rear. With royalist forces threatening, the 800 prisoners at La Guaira were an added source of trouble. Recalling his earlier disaster at Puerto Cabello, Bolívar ordered them shot, and the harsh order was carried out. Ribas repulsed Boves and his llanero lancers, but the patriots were nearly out of men and munitions, while the enemy forces daily grew larger as new recruits joined them.

The war had made Venezuela a desert, for thousands of people had been killed and the once-productive plantations were untilled and barren. "The war is becoming more cruel," Bolívar wrote, "and hopes of a prompt victory I had aroused in you have vanished. . . . One more effort and we shall destroy the enemies of the fatherland."

Assembling his troops at his San Mateo estate, Bolívar prepared to defend both Caracas and Valencia against Boves. At the eleventh hour Mariño came to his aid, and an all-day battle ended with Boves's withdrawal, but Campo Elías was killed. In May Bolívar defended Valencia against General Cagigal and an army of 5,000. The patriots attacked the royalists on the plain of Carabobo, but won only a Pyrrhic victory, for their losses and lack of weapons were so crippling they were unable to pursue and destroy the retreating enemy. If the patriots had immediately taken Puerto Cabello and attacked Boves before he had time to gather reinforcements, they might have ended the war. Instead they took time to celebrate the victory, while Bolívar enjoyed the company of Señorita Pepa.

The Second Republic staggered toward its fall, and news of Ferdinand's restoration convinced many patriots that there was no longer the slightest hope of victory. Apathy replaced enthusiasm. In an attempt to contain the royalists Bolívar sent Mariño to hold La Puerta, Urdaneta to harass Ceballos, and Jalón against Cagigal, leaving only a token force to defend Caracas. He was not prepared for the bad news that Boves and his llanero lancers were approaching La Puerta. Boves entered a small plain with a narrow pass at each end. Mariño had, therefore, a position easily defended against cavalry. Bolívar and his staff rushed to the scene, and he took command. Rashly advancing to the plain, Bolívar exposed his force to the skillful llanero lancers, who quickly cut it to pieces. The survivors fled in disorder to Caracas.

Boves entered Valencia, where he rewarded his Negro and zambo troops by allowing them to slaughter whites, both military and civilian. Boves himself set the tone of the victory celebration by ordering the women to assemble. Whip in hand, he forced the women to dance, while his men rounded up their husbands and brothers, drove them to the edge of the city, and lanced them to death. Boves found this sport so amusing he kept it up for several nights. Then, gathering more recruits from the lower classes, he marched confidently on Caracas.

Instead of joining Urdaneta and his army in the west, Bolívar withdrew to the east, followed by 20,000 miserable civilians. Although few of them would live to see Caracas again, their fate was hardly worse than that of their peers who remained in the city, for Boves unleashed his rapacious llaneros for an orgy of the sort they most enjoyed — rape, pillage, and murder. At Aragua llaneros overtook Bolívar, and killed 4,000 of the civilians who accompanied him. The unfortunate civilians were so terrified at the sound of Boves's name that at night they were frightened out of their wits by tree toads that made the woods echo with a sound resembling "Bo-vez."

The survivors fled to Cumaná. Before leaving Caracas Bolívar gathered twenty-four chests of silver and gems, mostly from the churches, and these were placed on a ship belonging to an Italian adventurer. Seeing that this admiral-pirate was preparing to sail with the chests, Bolívar and Mariño hastened on board in an effort to save the treasure and were taken to the island of Margarita. Those left behind in Cumaná felt treacherously deserted by cowardly leaders. Ribas and Piar declared Bolívar an outlaw.

When he and Mariño returned with such of the chests as they could salvage, no one believed their story. Ribas arrested Bolívar for desertion and seized the chests and weapons he had brought. Bolívar managed to convince his guards of his innocence, and they released him. Mariño, who declared that Bolívar "could have convinced stones of the necessity of his victory," accompanied him as he retraced his earlier steps to Cartagena.

After Bolívar and Mariño departed, the fighting continued in the east under the independent chieftains Ribas, Piar, and Bermúdez. Morales, with 6,000 men, cornered Bermúdez and 1,250 men in Maturín, but the defenders launched an offensive and won a surprising victory. Piar seized Cumaná, but refused to join forces with Ribas. Boves destroyed Piar's army and shot many of the Caracas refugees who had been unable to leave the country. Bermúdez and Ribas, on their way to attack Morales, learned of Piar's defeat. Bermúdez rashly pursued Boves, while Ribas returned to Maturín. Boves thrashed Bermúdez, who also fell back on Maturín. He and Ribas marched again after royalists, but Boves and Morales crushed them and scattered their forces. In this gloomy time for the patriots, there was only one bright spot — Boves, who was always where the fighting was heaviest, was killed by a patriot lancer. Morales, his second in command, succeeded him. Ribas tried to escape over the llanos, but was recognized and killed.

The death of Boves eliminated the patriots' most terrifying foe, and at the same time left the llaneros leaderless and adrift. Neither he nor the llaneros had actually fought for Spain: they simply fought against the patriots, but they had destroyed the Second Republic. Their extraordinary brutality had, however, greatly increased the hatred of Spain among the Creoles who survived.

In the west Urdaneta was gradually forced to withdraw into New Granada, but before leaving he sent several officers to Casanare to recruit and organize a cavalry force. One of the officers was a young llanero, José Antonio Páez, who would soon take Boves's place as leader of the plainsmen. (By that time, however, they would fight under the patriot banner.)

Undismayed by the calamities that had befallen him, Bolívar arrived at Cartagena in September, 1814. The campaign in Venezuela had failed, he explained, because he had counted on patriotism and enthusiasm that were lacking, and on a national spirit that did not exist and that he could not create. With a better understanding of all that was involved, he set out once more to liberate Venezuela with the aid of the Granadinos. He left Cartagena to address the Congress of the Allied Provinces in Tunja, where he was named captain general of the Colombian Federation and ordered to subdue the rebellious province of Cundinamarca. Antonio Nariño had been captured and sent to Spain in 1813, and his successor, Manuel Fernando Álvarez, was unenthusiastic about independence and hostile toward the confederation. Advancing swiftly, Bolívar took Bogotá, which was defended street by street, especially by the lower classes. Cudinamarca now entered the confederation under a guarantee of life and property of all citizens regardless of origin. Although there was some looting of homes, and the famous observatory was stripped of books and instruments, Bolívar was rewarded with the title of captain general of New Granada, the highest rank in the army.

Demanding sacrifices of both lives and fortunes, Bolívar

declared: "War is the epitome of all evil. But tyranny is the substance of all war." He ordered Urdaneta, whose army had reached Cúcuta, to defend New Granada against royalists from the east, and at the same time sent a force south toward the border of Ecuador. Because Álvarez had persuaded some of the *Peninsulares* in Bogotá to help defend the city, Bolívar proposed executing some who were related to prominent families, for he was certain they would cause trouble. Congress protested. "Tell them they shall be obeyed," Bolívar replied, "but that some day they will regret it. This country is unavoidably going to be occupied by the Spaniards, but never mind, I shall come again."

Once more divisions and jealousies among patriot commanders fatally undermined the independence movement. In January, 1815, Bolívar set out to occupy Santa Marta, for it was feared that new contingents of troops from Spain would land there, and he called on the independent state of Cartagena for assistance. His former rival and enemy, Colonel Castillo, commanded the army of Cartagena, and he not only rejected the request but published a scurrilous attack on Bolívar.

With Castillo and others working against him in Cartagena, Bolívar saw his plans completely upset. Royalist troops recovered control of the lower Magdalena and held most of the ports, and ships arriving from Spain brought fresh troops who were veterans of the campaigns against the French. Rather than precipitate a civil war at so critical a time Bolívar secured passage to Jamaica on a British warship, for in the face of hate, envy, jealousy, and greed, the independence struggle was hopeless. When Camilo Torres learned that Bolívar was in Jamaica, he said that he did not despair for his country — wherever Bolívar was, there the republic existed. And, as Daniel O'Leary pointed out, "very few have possessed to such a high degree as Bolívar the gift of inspiring noble sentiments and laudable enthusiasm in the hearts of others."

In May, 1815, General Pablo Morillo arrived with the largest army Spain had ever sent to the Americas — 11,000 well-equipped men. At Cumaná he met Morales, then continued on to Margarita, where Juan Bautista Arizmendi and Bermúdez commanded patriot forces. When the fleet approached they offered to surrender if forgiven for past acts. Morillo agreed. Bermúdez and 300 men escaped to Chacachacare, while Arizmendi, on his knees, asked Morillo to pardon him. Morales demanded that he be shot instead.

"I forgive him," Morillo said, and Arizmendi left.

"General," Morales said angrily, "I can now say that you will fail."

"I haven't asked you for advice," Morillo replied.

Leaving a small garrison on Margarita, Morillo sailed for Venezuela. At the island of Cocho, where the fleet anchored to take on water, the 74-gun warship *San Pedro* caught fire and its powder magazines exploded, killing 900 men. It was a serious loss, for in addition to the troops and seamen it contained most of Morillo's artillery, as well as rifles, ammunition, and uniforms. After this mishap Morillo sailed to La Guaira, entering Caracas in mid-May, shortly after Bolívar had left New Granada for Jamaica. He issued a proclamation to win over Venezuelans, then virtually repudiated it by sequestering the property of two-thirds of Venezuelan families, while his arrogance alienated the colored peoples who had previously been proroyalist.

Most of the troops Morillo brought were seasoned veterans, but many of the officers were unhappy with Ferdinand's tyranny and persecution of liberals. They had been told they were sailing for Buenos Aires and were shocked to learn that their destination was Venezuela, where the warfare was the bloodiest and atrocities were common. But it was a formidable army, and it struck the patriot cause a near-fatal blow.

In July Morillo landed at Santa Marta and sent Morales to lay siege to Cartagena. By the time the city fell in December, most of the people had starved to death and the streets were littered with corpses. Survivors such as Colonel Castillo paid for their obstinacy before firing squads or on the gibbet.

Within days after Cartagena fell Morillo was in Bogotá, where he allowed future viceroy Juan Sámano to conduct the "pacification," literally the systematic extermination of Granadino leaders. Camilo Torres, Rodríguez Torices, and dozens of others were shot, for anyone who could read and write was automatically deemed guilty of rebellion against the king. During this "year of the gallows" for New Granada, Morillo converted the country into a supply base for the royalist army in the north.

The year 1815 was the nadir of the Spanish-American wars of independence. Royalist control had been reestablished in Venezuela and New Granada in the north and in Chile in the south; it had never been seriously challenged in Peru and Ecuador. Chilean liberator Bernardo O'Higgins had fled across the Andes to Mendoza in western Argentina. Bolívar was in self-imposed exile in Jamaica. In Mexico both Miguel Hidalgo and José María Morelos had been captured and shot, their forces dispersed. Only in Argentina did patriot forces still hold out, but royalist armies were poised in Upper Peru to restore Ferdinand's authority in Buenos Aires, and royalist officers drank toasts to the coming victory.

But when royalist troops descended from the high, bleak altiplano to the lowlands of western Argentina, they were repulsed and routed by the gauchos of Salta, Tucumán, and Jujuy, the counterparts of the llaneros of Venezuela.

The patriots of the Río de la Plata were not reconquered, and in Mendoza General José de San Martín began building his Army of the Andes for the liberation of Chile and Peru.

In Jamaica Bolívar lived a precarious existence, supported by his English friend Maxwell Hyslop, who generously provided him with money whenever he needed it. On one occasion, after sharing a room with several other refugees, Bolívar found other quarters, and decided to remain there for the night without his baggage. Royalists had bribed Pío, an ex-slave, to assassinate him that very night. Pío stabbed to death the man who slept in Bolívar's hammock, but it was one of his friends, not the Liberator.

While in exile Bolívar wrote his famous "Letter from Jamaica," in which he expressed his feelings about the freedom of the Americas as well as his vision of their future. "The bonds that united us to Spain have been severed," he wrote. "The hatred which the Iberian Peninsula inspired in us is greater than the ocean which separates us. The War to the Death has done its work." The fact that he was in exile and the royalists had recovered control of the mainland made no difference as far as the eventual outcome was concerned. "A people that loves freedom," he wrote, "will in the end be free."

Turning to the matter of government, he continued: "As long as our fellow citizens do not acquire the talents and virtues which distinguish our brothers to the north, a radical democratic system, far from being good for us, will bring ruin upon us. Unfortunately we do not possess these traits. . . . We are ruled by corruption, which must be accepted under the rule of a country which had distinguished itself by inflexibility, ambition, vengeance, and greed." The Spanish-American states would need paternalistic governments to heal "the wounds and scars made by despotism and war." Quoting Rousseau, he said, "It is harder to free a nation from bondage than to enslave a free nation."

At the same time Bolívar made an oblique appeal to European nations, and particularly to Britain, by pointing out that those who supported Spanish-American independence would have a certain market for their goods. With British aid, he wrote, "we can shelter the rest of South America, and at the same time the provinces of Panamá and Nicaragua would be handed over to the British government, which could make these countries the center of world trade by opening canals that, by shortenening distances, would make the control of commerce by Britain permanent." But the British government had problems of its own at the moment, for Napoleon had escaped from Elba and was again exercising his military magic on the continent.

To Bolívar constant activity was as necessary as the companionship of women — if he was not actively involved in a campaign he was reading or planning or dictating scores of letters to his secretaries. He had an excellent memory, and he answered all correspondence. Four or five hours of sleep, in a hammock or wrapped in his cloak on the ground, sufficed him. An excellent horseman, he traveled greater distances on horseback than any other general before or since. In this he was the equal of the toughest llaneros, who in admiration gave him virtually the same nickname George Armstrong Custer's men would later bestow on him — *culo de hierro* (iron ass).

Although he was an urbane, aristocratic officer, when necessary Bolívar lived the hard life of the llanero. He was a warrior, a fighter, rather than a military genius or cunning strategist, and he learned the art of war on campaign rather than from military treatises. In battle he was active, quick, and violent, and his unrestrained ardor brought him victory or catastrophe. "I am the son of war," he once said. "War is my element — danger my glory."

Early in December Bolívar received news that Castillo had been deposed and an invitation to return to Cartagena as commander in chief, for the city was still holding out against Morales. Bolívar accepted the offer, but while at sea met a schooner whose captain informed him that Cartagena had fallen. He turned instead to Haiti, which had won its independence from France in 1804.

THREE

Angostura to Bogotá

ON JANUARY 2, 1816, shortly after Bolívar landed at Port-au-Prince, President Alexandre Pétion received him cordially. An ex-slave who had served in the French army before joining the Haitian rebellion, Pétion acknowledged Bolívar as the foremost liberator of the continent. Bolívar's decision to seek aid in Haiti had far-reaching consequences, for it committed slave owner Bolívar to abolish slavery and to uphold equality between blacks and whites in the lands he might free from Spanish rule. Pétion made emancipation of slaves a condition for providing the sinews of war. Bolívar wanted to give Pétion credit for all future abolition decrees, but he modestly declined the honor.

"You know my sentiments for the cause whose defense you have undertaken," he said, "and my personal feelings for you. You must be permeated with the knowledge of how keenly I wish that all who suffer under the yoke of slavery be freed." Because Haiti itself was in a difficult situation, Pétion's assistance was covert, through Bolívar's friend Robert Sutherland, an English merchant.

Many Venezuelan refugees were already in Haiti, including Mariño, Piar, Bermúdez, and Leandro Palacios, and others continued to arrive. Luis Brión, a wealthy Creole from Curaçao who owned or chartered a number of armed vessels, joined the group and devoted himself and his wealth to the cause of Spanish-American independence. "Admiral Brión has a shrine of gratitude in every Colombian heart," Bolívar commented in 1821, after learning of Brión's death. Louis Aury, a Frenchman who also had a number of ships and who had taken part in the defense of Cartagena, also arrived. A Scot, Gregor MacGregor, and another Frenchman, H. L. V. Ducoudray-Holstein, joined the refugees.

When the patriots assembled, Bolívar presided and spoke of the need for a strong, central government. There was some discussion of a triumvirate, but Bolívar opposed any division of power as dangerous to the cause. The debate ended when Brión proposed that Bolívar be named commander in chief, adding that he would provide ships and credit to Bolívar, but to none other. When he asked Mariño and the others individually if they would support Bolívar, they glumly acquiesced; ambition to command was shared by all.

Bolívar wrote out the powers he was to have — some said that he had already prepared them before the meeting — and insisted that each sign the articles. Aury refused to sign the article giving Bolívar dictatorial powers and withdrew from the expedition. Bolívar named Ducoudray-Holstein chief of staff, Brión admiral of the republic, and Francisco Antonio Zea chief administrator. Opposition to Bolívar, petty rivalries, and general irritation led to disputes and to four challenges to duels. Finally Pétion ended the factionalism by announcing that those who did not sail with Bolívar would not be allowed to depart.

The departure was delayed by quarrels and lack of favorable winds; and, according to Ducoudray-Holstein, it was delayed an additional forty-eight hours while Señorita Pepa and her mother and sister were brought from the island of San Beata. Some men were so irate over the delay they quit the expedition and went ashore. The others sailed in six schooners and a sloop — 250 men, mostly officers, and arms for 6,000 troops. They sailed to Margarita, which Arizmendi had retaken from the royalists in the interim. The Spanish brig *Intrépido* and schooner *Rita* blockaded the island, but the patriot squadron captured both. Arizmendi and his junta acknowledged Bolívar as Supreme Chief of the Republic and Mariño as second-in-command.

Late in May the expedition landed at Carúpano in eastern Venezuela, defeated the royalist garrison there, and captured a valuable store of arms and ammunition. Mariño and Piar asked Bolívar for weapons and permission to seek recruits in the east. Even though he knew their real purpose was to be free of his authority, Bolívar agreed. They sent him 200 recruits, but they did not return even when ordered to do so. Bolívar freed the slaves in the area on condition they join his army. Several hundred joined the patriots, but the majority of ex-slaves went over to the royalists.

In July Bolívar landed his troops at Ocumare, between La Guaira and Puerto Cabello, expecting Venezuelans to rally to his colors and enable him to march to the heart of the country. In this he was disappointed, as Miranda had been a decade earlier, for he met only apathy. He proclaimed the War to the Death ended, and decreed an end to slavery. "Henceforth," he said, "there shall be in Venezuela only one class of men: all will be citizens." Emancipation alienated slave owners, but most of the people were more frightened than apathetic, for the "Man of Terror," Morales, was in command in Venezuela — and the War to the Death did not end. Morales defeated General Carlos Soublette, whose rank was largely a reward for his sister's favors to Bolívar, rather than for demonstrated skill on the battlefield. The campaign had been doomed from the outset, for Bolívar had overestimated the Venezuelans' patriotic fervor and had underestimated the obstacles. His officers urged him to sail as Morales approached, saying they would battle their way to the llanos. There was panic and confusion, and some men believed that Bolívar had been distracted by a woman at a crucial time. As Soublette put it, "Marc Antony, unmindful of the danger in which he found himself, lost valuable time at Cleopatra's side." When Morales entered Ocumare, he found that the town had been abandoned.

The panic had been caused by the report of Bolívar's aide, Isidro Alzuru, that Morales was already in Ocumare, although Soublette had sent Alzuru to inform Bolívar that Morales was camped in woods near the town and that Soublette's troops had the camp covered, awaiting Bolívar's orders. Bolívar's officers begged him to save himself, and he hastened to board the last ship as its cables were being cut, leaving his army without instructions and abandoning most of the arms. Alzuru informed Soublette that Bolívar had sailed before he arrived. Then Alzuru defected to the royalists. This mishap brought Bolívar more bitter criticism than anything else, although Soublette saved the munitions or threw them into the sea. Bolívar tried to persuade the ship captain to land him at the nearby port of Choroni so he could rejoin his army, but the captain sailed for the island of Bonaire.

On the following day Bolívar returned to the coast with Brión, but they found the royalists in control and learned that the patriots had withdrawn to the interior under command of MacGregor. Bolívar was fortunate to survive the Ocumare calamity, for Mariño, Bermúdez, and other rivals considered it an excellent opportunity to terminate his command. When he joined them in Güiria, therefore, they refused to acknowledge his authority.

There was nothing for Bolívar to do but depart; Bermúdez would deny him even that alternative, and he had to fight his way to the shore, sword in hand. To avoid civil war, he returned to Port-au-Prince to seek Pétion's help once more.

One of Bolívar's most valuable assets for his chosen task was his stubborn macho spirit that never conceded defeat, for his strength of character enabled him to rise above any disaster. Morillo, with grudging admiration, declared that Bolívar was more terrible in defeat than in victory. When he suffered a reverse he quickly replaced his losses and returned to win victories. Each experience, whether triumph or disaster, simply added to his strength and determination. He was dedicated to freedom, and he was absolutely certain that he was destined to bring it to Spanish Americans. Knowing without any doubt that he would eventually triumph, at the darkest moments, when his companions were sunk in gloom, he was looking ahead, making what seemed at the moment grandiose plans.

Pétion received him with warmth and respect, for he had known similar trials and he sensed that Bolívar was a man of destiny. Even the most ambitious Venezuelan patriots also recognized Bolívar's unrivaled keenness of mind and willpower and leadership. There was now a reaction in his favor, and during a war council MacGregor's officers and most of the others voted to restore him as commander in chief and to send Colonel Francisco Antonio Zea to Haiti with the invitation. In December, 1816, Bolívar sailed once more to resume the struggle, taking a liberal supply of arms and ammunition supplied by Pétion, and accompanied by some French and British officers.

Mariño, Piar, Bermúdez, and MacGregor had been active in the six months since the catastrophe at Ocumare. They held the peninsula of Paria, from which they made sorties against royalist garrisons in Cumaná province. MacGregor, following Bolívar's plan for penetrating royalist lines, had reached the southwest and joined forces with other patriot guerrilla units under Pedro Zaraza and José Tadeo Monagas. On the way he defeated a number of royalist detachments. After the first victory he refused to allow the shooting of prisoners, releasing them when he moved on. In less than five miles he saw forty Creoles whose throats had been cut by a company of Catalans. Before he reached his destination, his army had doubled in size, the recruits being 200 Indians and 600 llaneros. With this force he inflicted heavy losses on the royalists who held Barcelona and wrested the city from them. MacGregor's campaign was one of the most daring and successful of the wars.

In Barcelona he reorganized his army, now strengthened by other patriot units, and prepared to meet Morales. Piar hurried to join him. Together they met the larger royalist force on the plains of Juncal, and sent it reeling westward with heavy casualties. Because of differences with Piar, MacGregor left the Venezuelan service. Morales meanwhile vented his anger by killing unarmed civilians.

Bolívar, who joined the patriots in Barcelona, learned of an effective guerrilla force in the west under llanero José Antonio Páez. Earlier in the year Páez, with 400 llaneros, had defeated 1,500 royalists under Colonel Rafael López, a victory that made him the idol of the plainsmen.

General Morillo, worried about the possible loss of the strategic province of Guayana, returned to Venezuela during the month before Bolívar reached Barcelona. He sent

Miguel de la Torre across the mountains, where he met Páez with 1,300 llaneros and felt fortunate to escape. But Morillo routed Bolívar, who had only 700 men, and threatened Barcelona, where most of the patriots' supplies were stored.

Bolívar urged the various independent chieftains to hurry to the defense of Barcelona. Piar ignored the summons, but Mariño arrived in January, 1817, with 1,200 men. Meanwhile Piar had undertaken the conquest of Guayana; it now occurred to Bolívar that this region was the most strategic base for his operations, for whoever held the province and plains would eventually control all of Venezuela.

Without an army of his own (except for 600 Indians armed with bows and arrows), Bolívar had to court the various chieftains who had personal followings. He won over Bermúdez, but Mariño and Piar remained aloof. Páez did not question his authority, but accepted it with reservations. Bolívar knew that a permanent government was necessary for the reconstruction of Venezuela, which meant finding a location impenetrable by royalists. The Orinoco region and Guayana plains were ideal, for llanero cavalry could make the plains untenable for royalist infantry, and the Orinoco provided a reliable avenue for vital supplies. The region also had products that could be traded for munitions. When he marched to the interior, Bolívar had all of the supplies that could not be carried shipped to Margarita to prevent them from falling into royalist hands. He left a small force to hold Barcelona, requesting Mariño to reinforce it.

José Joaquín Cortés Madariaga, who was on Margarita writing a constitution, informed Bolívar that Britain would soon recognize the independence of some of the new Spanish-American nations, but only those that possessed "organized governments with forces and resources capable of enforcing respect for their liberties." For this reason Cortés Madariaga insisted on the need to reestablish the government with "its legitimate division of powers," for otherwise "we shall be held in contempt by the world and fall prey to anarchy." He repeated an earlier warning to Bolívar that "force is not government."

Crossing to Cariaco on the mainland, Cortés Madariaga discussed with Mariño, Brión, Zea, and others the need for a "regular government." Mariño assured some that Bolívar had approved the plan for government, which was nothing more than a conspiracy to give Mariño supreme power. Bolívar was to be merely a member of a three-man executive committee, while Mariño would be commander in chief. Carried away by the role of creator, the group decided that members of congress should be addressed as "Honorable," members of the executive committee as "Respectable," members of the judiciary as "Upright," and the captain general and admiral as "Honorable" only as a courtesy. They now called on Brión to provide ships to move them and their families to Maturín.

By this time, however, the Honorable Admiral realized that he had erred in supporting Mariño's ambitions. He replied that on orders from the "Supreme Chief" he could take them only to Guayana, which was under Bolívar's control. There was no Supreme Chief called for in the constitution, but, as José Yáñez remarked, with Brión's reply "the general government stood dissolved." The whole affair was ridiculous, but by example it did much harm to the patriots. A number of officers, including Rafael Urdaneta and Colonel Antonio José de Sucre, quickly trimmed their sails and set course for Guayana, to serve under Bolívar. Mariño had refused to aid in the defense of Barcelona, and royalists under Colonel Juan Aldama took the city in April, putting to the sword all of the patriot garrison as well as the civilians who had taken refuge with the troops. Mariño's defection was lamentable, but few troops or officers accompanied him.

When Brión sailed up the Orinoco, Bolívar and a few officers went to meet him. The royalists somehow learned of the journey and laid an ambush for Bolívar on his return, a trap that very nearly succeeded. That same night, while his companions thought only of saving their lives, Bolívar vowed he would liberate New Granada, create a Gran Colombia by uniting it with Venezuela, and carry the patriot banner to Lima and Potosí. Although his friends thought he had gone mad, it was no idle boast.

During the siege of Angostura Bolívar established his headquarters on an inlet of the Orinoco, about ten miles from the city, where his troops were building launches to be used against the royalists. A royalist force surprised them. Bolívar, Soublette, and others escaped by dashing across the inlet. General Arizmendi, who could not swim, waded until the water was over his head. When a servant rescued him, his companions asked why he had entered the water when he could not swim. "If it had been boiling lead," Arizmendi replied, "I should have done the same rather than fall into the power of the Spaniards, dead or alive." Last to cross to safety was Bolívar's servant, Dionisio, whose progress was delayed by the machete he carried. When asked why he had taken such risk to save the huge knife, he replied that he meant to kill Bolívar with it rather than allow the royalists to capture him.

In May Piar laid siege to Angostura, the key city on the Orinoco. In July the royalists abandoned it and sailed downriver, where Piar's troops and Brión's squadron killed or captured most of them. Piar ordered 180 Spaniards, including the governor of Angostura, shot in reprisal for their own atrocities. This royalist disaster gave Bolívar the base he needed; as long as he controlled the Orinoco he had access to the sea and, therefore, to supplies as well as foreign recruits. From this time on, the patriot campaigns were better organized and more systematic, and although the patriots suffered defeats, they always had a base to fall back to for rebuilding.

General Morillo was obsessed with the reconquest of Margarita, which he undertook himself in July, while assigning the defense of Guayana to La Torre. With 2,600 men General José de Canterac had brought from Spain for use in Peru, Morillo landed on Margarita, where he suffered heavy losses. When he learned that the patriots had overrun Guayana, he seized this as an excuse to withdraw from Margarita and sail for La Guaira on his way to Caracas. He admitted that the people of Margarita "were endowed with superhuman courage, possessed of the strength of giants." From Caracas he marched to Calabozo, the gateway to the llanos, and established his headquarters there in hope of preventing Páez from joining Bolívar.

Although Bolívar had secured control of the Orinoco, it was only one step in his program, for he had yet to unite the various patriot guerrilla forces into an army that could cope with the royalists in conventional warfare. Piar consistently refused to acknowledge Bolívar's authority, for he was dissatisfied with his secondary role and considered the Orinoco region his by right of conquest and Bolívar an interloper. In vain Bolívar tried to soothe him and pleaded with him to cooperate in the patriot cause, but he clung tenaciously to his independent command. Piar was an excellent fighter and had thrashed La Torre and other professional royalist officers with much larger forces than his own. But Bolívar realized that he could not launch a major campaign from Angostura while Piar was at his back and beyond his authority. Piar's continued independence, furthermore, encouraged deviation on the part of Mariño and other patriot chieftains such as Páez. Bolívar realized that he must take drastic action to pacify and unify the patriot commanders before the patriot forces disintegrated into a series of minor and warring factions.

When Bermúdez informed him Piar was planning a rebellion, Bolívar acted quickly and decisively. He ordered Piar to report to headquarters, adding that he would be arrested and brought there if he refused. Piar fled to the east, where it was feared he would join Mariño. But a cavalry detachment overtook him and brought him to Angostura. He demanded to see Bolívar, but was refused.

A war council now charged Piar with desertion, insurrection, and treason, and Brión presided over his court-martial. The sentence was demotion and death. To the surprise of many, Bolívar rejected demotion but did not commute the death sentence, although he was reminded of Piar's many achievements. Fearful of an uprising on the day of the execution, Bolívar nevertheless ordered the sentence carried out as an object lesson to others.

Because Piar was a mulatto some historians have accused Bolívar of racial hatred as well as envy and hunger for power. The charge of racism is unjustified, but Bolívar was certainly not immune to envy. Piar was a disruptive element and would-be rival who overestimated his power, and it was for this he was eliminated. Because the unfortunate Piar was executed, other independent chiefs hastened to become reconciled with Bolívar, and the patriot cause was greatly strengthened as a result. As Bolívar commented: "The death of General Piar was a political necessity which saved the country. The rebels were disturbed and frightened. . . . Mariño and his congress in Cariaco were dismissed. All came under my command. . . . Never was there a death more useful, more politic, and at the same time more deserved." He added that "General Mariño also deserved to die. But he was not so dangerous; in his case policy could give way to humanity." It should be added that Piar was not a Venezuelan but Mariño was, so that it would have been far more risky to make an object lesson of Mariño than of Piar.

Mariño was quickly isolated and replaced by Bermúdez as commander of Cumaná. Bolívar ordered him to come to Angostura and swear allegiance to the government, in which case the past would be forgotten. Aware that he had gone too far, Mariño meekly yielded. Bolívar was now in full control, and had achieved two of his goals. The defeat of the royalists was still in the future, but he now had a secure base for operations, and he was confident of eventual success.

Morillo had become discouraged by the patriots' occupation of Guayana, and his ablest officers were ill or recovering from wounds. His supplies were insufficient and his forces were composed largely of natives of Venezuela and New Granada, which made him doubt their reliability. He could not destroy Bolívar's forces in the Orinoco region, and in western Venezuela Páez had proved unconquerable. To Morillo, in fact, Páez and his llanero lancers were more to be feared than Bolívar's army.

Páez was a typical llanero, thoroughly inured to the harsh life on the Venezuelan llanos — even when he rose to the rank of general he had not learned to eat with knife and fork. But he understood the llaneros, who called him "Tio Antonio" — Uncle Anthony — and followed him without hesitation. As a leader of guerrilla cavalry he was unsurpassed. Like Boves he was always in the thick of the fighting, accompanied by his huge bodyguard, El Negro Primero (Number One Negro), an ex-slave who had gone to war to secure shirts for himself and two friends, and who saved Páez countless times. Páez was subject to epileptic seizures during battles, and El Negro Primero carried him to safety or stood over him.

Before leaving Angostura Bolívar appointed a council

of state composed of Brión, Zea, and Manuel Cedeño — a council which had advisory functions only. He sent most of his army under Zaraza to delay Morillo's approach and to prevent a surprise attack on patriot headquarters. Although Zaraza's orders were explicit — restrict all activity to defense and evasion — early in December, 1817, he met La Torre's army in an open area called La Hogaza and risked all in a full-scale battle. The result was a disaster for the patriots; the losses of both men and arms were staggering. Because of this catastrophe Bolívar had to alter his plans, reorganize his army, fill the depleted ranks with conscripts, and send for arms. Morillo, after the battle of La Hogaza, commented that "a victorious Bolívar goes a way that can be reasoned out, but a defeated Bolívar is more active and terrible than ever, and no one can tell where he will break out." When he said this he thought Bolívar was still in Angostura, but the Liberator and his subordinates had raised and equipped a new expeditionary force in three weeks. Although it was inadequately armed and trained, its officers were veterans of many campaigns. Bermúdez was to command the troops while Mariño was sent to harass the enemy along the eastern coast. Zaraza was sent to the Barcelona plains to raise a cavalry force to threaten Caracas and distract Morillo.

With the guerrilla forces of Monagas and Cedeño, Bolívar crossed the Orinoco and marched more than 600 miles, during which the army had to cross many rivers. At the end of January, 1818, they reached the Apure and found Páez. The combined armies now numbered 3,000 men, but of 2,000 infantry, only 1,400 had guns. At the meeting with Páez Bolívar raised the question of getting his troops across the Río Apure, for the only *flecheras,* or riverboats, were those of the royalists on the opposite shore. "I shall provide them," Páez assured Bolívar.

"Where from?" Páez pointed to the royalist crafts across

the river, then selected fifty of his men. "We must take those *flecheras* or die," he exclaimed. "Let those who wish follow their Uncle." The llaneros, lances held high, spurred their horses into the river, routed the royalists, and captured fourteen *flecheras*. Páez was both fearless and resourceful as a guerrilla leader, and though not cruel, was careless about human life. According to O'Leary, his dominant passion was power. He called Páez "rash, active, brave, fertile in ruses, quick in imagination, resolute in execution, rapid in his movements, the weaker the force he commanded, the more terrible he was."

When Morillo learned that Bolívar and Páez had joined forces on the Apure, he moved quickly to save Calabozo, but Bolívar inflicted heavy losses on him the day after he arrived. The following day Bolívar offered to exchange prisoners and to end the War to the Death. Morillo did not reply, but Bolívar ordered an end to the shooting of prisoners. Bolívar camped six or seven miles from Calabozo, leaving a regiment of hussars to watch Morillo. Under cover of night Morillo abandoned Calabozo, and owing to the laxness of the hussars made good his escape. In the morning the hussars reported the flight to Bolívar without seeing which road the royalists had taken. Bolívar sent a force of cavalry after him, but as it had to go first to Calabozo to find his trail, he had time to find refuge at Valencia. Morillo had made a forced march, wasting no time on stragglers, with the result that he lost 800 men. But had the hussars performed their duty, he probably would have been captured. Such laxness and lack of discipline were frequent among cavalry leaders. Bolívar's march to Calabozo and surprise of Morillo, and the latter's retreat, were both brilliant feats.

The patriots now faced the choice between advancing on Caracas, as Bolívar desired, or going into winter quarters at Calabozo. Páez and other llanero chiefs refused to march on Caracas, for their lancers preferred to remain in familiar country, hated discipline, and were prone to desertion. They understood the meaning of liberty but had only vague notions about independence.

Bolívar argued with Páez but in vain, for they held totally different concepts concerning conduct of the war. Bolívar wanted to seek out the royalist forces and destroy them in an all-out battle, while Páez preferred to grind them down by guerrilla warfare, the only tactics he knew. Without a sufficient army of his own Bolívar had no choice but to return to Calabozo, while Páez took his llaneros to drive the royalists from San Fernando.

Because inactivity led to mass desertions, Bolívar and his war council concluded that they must launch a new campaign before the army disintegrated completely. He wrote Páez to hasten his operations against San Fernando, for "we shall not obtain a decisive advantage until we are all together working as a single unit." Early in March the campaign began, and Bolívar was soon joined by Monagas with a cavalry brigade. Urdaneta argued in favor of gaining complete control of the llanos, so they could count on the llaneros. Cedeño and others favored marching to the Valle de Aragua, and their view prevailed.

From a captured royalist courier Bolívar learned that La Torre was approaching with three divisions. Monagas, with his cavalry and the Angostura battalion, checked the royalist vanguard under Morales while Bolívar prepared a defensive position at El Semen. The royalists attacked repeatedly but were repulsed, while Bolívar, accompanied by Monagas and a small cavalry escort, directed the fighting. The outcome of the battle was undecided until Colonel Genaro Vásquez and dismounted cavalrymen charged the royalists with lances. In the rout that followed Morillo suffered a lance wound and was forced to surrender command temporarily. When Bolívar had suggested ending the War to the Death Morillo had felt insulted. When he was wounded, however, he ordered General Correa to respect the lives of prisoners taken at El Semen. After recovering from his wound, though, he again ordered prisoners shot. Both sides had suffered extremely heavy losses — Bolívar lost most of his infantry as well as equipment and his papers. Among the patriots wounded were generals Urdaneta, Manuel Valdés, Manuel Torres, and José Antonio Anzoátegui. There was nothing for the patriots to do but fall back to Calabozo and rebuild the army.

From Calabozo Bolívar and his staff and a cavalry escort set out to join Páez and Cedeño, while La Torre with 1,500 infantry marched to Ortiz. As usual the royalists could not fathom Bolívar's amazing recuperative powers, for La Torre supposed that he had given up after the costly battle at El Semen. Yet in little more than a week after El Semen Bolívar attacked La Torre at Ortiz. The hastily recruited patriot infantry tried for six hours to dislodge the royalists, but their position was too strong. When the fighting ended, nevertheless, La Torre quickly withdrew to the Valle de Aragua, leaving wounded and prisoners behind. Bolívar fell back to San Pablo, sending Soublette to Guayana to obtain arms.

In April, a month after El Semen, a royalist force under Colonel López learned that Bolívar was camped at El Rincón de los Toros. A patriot deserter provided the password, and a select force under Captain Tomás Renovales was sent to kill or capture Bolívar. When Colonel Santander challenged them Renovales gave the password and said that they were looking for the Supreme Chief. Santander called to Bolívar, who leaped from his hammock and escaped, although other officers were less fortunate. With a few troops Bolívar reached Calabozo, where he was immediately as energetic as ever in rebuilding his army once more. He learned that Páez, too, had suffered a costly defeat, at Cojedes in one of the bloodiest battles of the war. As a result the royalists occupied the llanos as far as Calabozo. The patriot cause was at another low point, worse than at the beginning of the year, for the royalists now held all of the major cities.

From June to December, 1818, Bolívar was in Angostura planning new strategy while tirelessly training an army for yet another campaign. Since most of the men in both royalist and patriot armies were Venezuelans, the war was rapidly depopulating the land, making recruiting difficult. Most of the survivors were proroyalists who fled at the sight of patriot troops. Seasoned infantry regiments from Spain formed the nucleus of the royalist army while Bolívar's infantry was composed of untrained youths from fourteen to twenty years old. To counter the Spanish veterans he had ordered López Méndez, who was still in London, to recruit British troops.

Because of a depression in Britain and the reduction of the army, López Méndez was able to acquire both men and arms. All officers who joined were promised a promotion and the same pay as in the British service. Although López Méndez could offer only promissory notes, the legend of El Dorado was still strong, and British merchants with warehouses full of arms were happy to accept the notes. By the end of 1817 five regiments prepared to sail, 800 men in all, with the best weapons and equipment. One regiment was lost when its ship sank during a storm, and in the West Indies many men deserted, but in the spring of 1818, 150 Britishers reached Guayana. An Irish regiment as well as some Germans who had served under the Duke of Wellington also arrived. Eventually 4,000 Europeans, including Spaniards, joined Bolívar's army. Their scarlet uniforms, which quickly went to pieces in the tropics, at first made a bizarre contrast to the rags and nakedness of the tough llaneros. Some of the foreign soldiers were placed in mixed regiments, so that Venezuelans would learn the tactics and discipline of the Europeans, while the latter learned to endure the hardships that were part of life for the natives. In this way Bolívar eventually built up a fighting force that would carry him to victory.

At the moment, however, he was in Apure trying to recruit Venezuelans, leaving Soublette in Angostura to receive the arms shipments Brión was sending from the islands. Páez controlled San Fernando, and he won over some of the British officers, persuading them and his own to draw up a statement declaring him commander in chief of the patriot army. Páez was confident that he was safe from retaliation, but like Mariño and others before him he underestimated Bolívar's resourcefulness, determination, and courage. Bolívar arrested one of the British officers who had defected, and ordered Páez to send the documents necessary for his prosecution. Recalling Piar's fate, Páez destroyed the declaration naming him commander in chief.

The mercurial nature and unreliability of his supposed subordinate chiefs obliged Bolívar to rely increasingly on foreign officers. A stream of British ships brought uniforms and munitions as well as recruits. Some of the officers demanded payments he could not make, and U.S. diplomatic agent J. B. Irvine insisted on immediate compensation for two American ships the patriots had captured while they were carrying provisions to royalists besieged in Angostura the previous year. When Bolívar agreed to accept only arbitration of the dispute, Irvine threatened U.S. retaliation against Venezuela, a ridiculous gesture that was brushed aside.

Although Bolívar received offers of help from Spanish officers such as Renovales, who had been exiled from Spain for their liberal principles, most Venezuelans had gone over to the royalists. Even some of Bolívar's own relatives had taken refuge in royalist areas, and Señorita Pepa and her mother and sister were in Caracas, where they remained despite his efforts to entice them to Angostura.

The effect of the strenuous campaigns on Bolívar was noted by Colonel G. Hippisley, one of the British officers.

I had a full opportunity of surveying the general whilst he was in conversation. . . . From what I had heard of him I was led to expect a very different man. . . . General Bolívar is a mean-looking person seemingly . . . about fifty years in age [Bolívar was actually thirty-four at the time]. He is about 5 feet, 6 inches in height; thin, sallow complexion, lengthened visage, marked with every symptom of anxiety and care, I could almost add, despondency. He seemed to have undergone great fatigue, his dark and, according to report, brilliant eyes, were now dull and heavy. . . . In my eyes he might have passed for anything but the thing he really was. Across the chamber was suspended one of the Spanish hammocks on which he occasionally sat, lolled and swang whilst conversing and seldom remained in the same posture for two minutes together. . . . The general-in-chief is, in common with the rest of his countrymen, much attached to women, and one, two or three generally accompany him on his various marches.

Bolívar still hoped to liberate Caracas, but he heard rumors that San Martín, who had organized and led an army across the Andes to free Chile, planned to invade Peru next. The news suddenly inspired Bolívar to think of driving the royalists out of New Granada and then marching on Ecuador and Peru. He sent Santander with a force to take command of guerrilla units in the province of Casanare in eastern New Granada, to recruit an army, and to harass the royalists in western Venezuela and eastern New Granada. Santander also carried Bolívar's proclamation to the people of New Granada, to inform them he was coming.

At Fernando Peñalver's urging, Bolívar determined to convene a congress at Angostura, even at the risk of a lessening of his dictatorial powers, which had caused so much resentment and opposition. The Council of State, presumably an advisory body, was, as O'Leary remarked, merely "a meeting of civil servants and military officers appointed by the chief with no other power than that of discussing some of the affairs which he had already settled." Those around Bolívar naturally resented being relegated to the role of puppets.

Peñalver's advice was sound, as Bolívar soon realized and later admitted. "You were the man," he wrote,

> who urged me most insistently to set up the Congress of Angostura, which gave me a greater reputation than all my past services, for men want to be served in a way that pleases everybody, and the way to please them is to invite them to share in the power and glory of command. I know full well that you contributed to the burial of all my enemies, whom I buried alive in the Congress of Angostura, for from that day they lost their jealousy and virulence; and to be sure, you were the only one who advised me to take such a step.

He summoned the Council of State and suggested that its members establish a committee to decide how to conduct the election of delegates to a congress. It was not enough, he told them, for the armies to be victorious — they needed "to be free under the auspices of liberal laws emanating from the most sacred spring . . . the will of the people."

The creation of a government in the little tropical town

of Angostura on the Orinoco, out of a population with no tradition of self-government and little sense of compromise, was a remarkable feat. To hold elections of delegates was no simple matter, for the destructive war had left chaos and disorder everywhere. Bolívar wanted thirty-five delegates, but only twenty-six reached Angostura by February, 1819. When they assembled for the first time, Bolívar addressed them in one of his most impressive speeches.

"The first day of my peace will be the last day of my power," he promised the delegates, and he warned them of the dangers of giving unlimited power to any man. "He becomes accustomed to command, the people become accustomed to obey. Usurpation and tyranny are the results." Knowing that the delegates had no experience in constitution-writing, Bolívar pointed out that the duty of the congress was to find a formula which expressed the major virtues of the complete state — maximum happiness, social security, and political stability.

Praising the British government as a model, he warned that the U.S. government should not be copied, because conditions there were vastly different from those in Venezuela. He cited Montesquieu's dictum that laws must conform to the spirit of the nation. He especially feared an attempt to revive federalism, which in Venezuela meant only anarchy. He favored an upper house with hereditary membership, like the British House of Lords, to offset the freely elected representatives. Bolívar had no confidence in the masses; he preferred a conservative republic administered by an intellectual and moral elite.

The presidency he envisaged was an absolute monarchy without the trappings of royalty, with a Creole elite serving as a governing nobility. His goal was political stability, with as much individual liberty as could be afforded without the threat of anarchy. "Venezuelans love their country," he said, "but they do not love its laws." Bolívar also saw the need for a fourth power of government, to improve popular morality and purge the nation of the corruption and degeneration spread by the war. But he knew that a strong government was most urgent, and other things could wait. "Let us not attempt the impossible," he advised the lawmakers. "If we rise too high in the sphere of liberty, we shall again fall into the abyss of tyranny. Unity, Unity, Unity — that must ever be our motto!"

He concluded by presenting his idea of a Gran Colombia formed by union between Venezuela and New Granada, a nucleus that he hoped would eventually encompass all of the new Spanish-American states. Laying aside his speech, he said, "Gentlemen, begin your tasks. I have completed mine." Deafening applause mingled with vivas for Venezuela followed.

Francisco Antonio Zea was elected provisional president of the convention. Zea was a Granadino, a famous botanist who had served as director of the botanic gardens of Madrid, and he was one of the Spaniards who had gone to France to labor on Napoleon's Bayonne Constitution of 1808. After Zea took the oath of office, Bolívar addressed his officers, informing them that he and they were now ordinary citizens, and the congress could confirm them in their ranks or reject them. For added emphasis he handed Zea his marshal's baton, symbol of authority. "I return to the Republic the baton of marshal it had entrusted to me. To serve her, any class or rank that Congress may confer on me will be for me an honor; in it I shall give the example of subordination and the blind obedience that must distinguish every soldier of the Republic." It was an ostentatious, theatrical gesture, made to impress insubordinate chieftains such as Páez and Mariño. Zea immediately compared Bolívar to a galaxy of the greatest Roman emperors, asking the congress if it would let him leave without investing him with the same authority he had surrendered. He was, of course, immediately and noisily reinstated.

On the following day the congress elected Bolívar President of the Republic. Modestly arguing that he lacked the necessary administrative qualities, he declared his only desire was to share the dangers and honors with his army. The congress, as might be expected, insisted, and Bolívar patriotically bowed to its demands. Zea was chosen vice-president, to serve in Bolívar's place when military duties preoccupied him.

The Congress of Angostura was an astute move, for it gave Bolívar a secure, official status while depriving his rivals of legitimate grounds for complaint. It also demonstrated to foreign nations that Venezuela was united as well as independent, a state deserving recognition, and some began taking notice of Venezuela for the first time. Bolívar was no longer simply a rebel chieftain and self-proclaimed dictator, though he still retained dictatorial powers. As president of the new nation, he now towered above his ambitious rivals. It was no empty boast that he had buried all of his opponents at the Congress of Angostura.

That no one accused Bolívar of theatrical opportunism was a tribute to his performance. Colonel J. P. Hamilton, who observed the proceedings, declared rather extravagantly that "General Bolívar gave a proof of his modesty and patriotism such as cannot be found in the history of any country." What Bolívar had demonstrated most of all, however, was his intellectual superiority to all other independence leaders. His work in Angostura done, he left to rejoin his army on the Apure.

While Bolívar was in Angostura Morillo was in Calabozo, gateway to the llanos, with 7,000 men, hoping to drive Bolívar out of the region into better terrain for conventional warfare. He crossed the Arauca after Páez about the time Bolívar rejoined the llanero chief early in March. Bolívar, who would have preferred a single, decisive battle, now had to adopt Páez's guerrilla tactics to weaken the royalist army. His infantrymen, who were still inferior to those of the royalists, he placed on islands, where they were safe from attack and well supplied with beef cattle. Llanero lancers lured the royalists into swamps and burned the grass where the royalist cavalry was camped, to weaken its horses. Morillo, seeing that he could not cope with the guerrilla tactics, withdrew to the Apure.

Now the patriots had to become the pursuers. In one encounter Páez deceived Morillo into believing that the whole patriot army was before him and ordering a cavalry charge. The llaneros pretended flight until the royalists were strung out in pursuit, then turned on them and killed 400. There were many smaller engagements, all raising patriot morale. As his losses continued to mount, Morillo crossed the Apure to set up winter quarters.

Still obsessed with the desire to liberate Caracas, Bolívar decided to assemble an army in eastern Venezuela, then cooperate with Páez and Cedeño. On his way to Mariño's headquarters in November, 1818, he learned that Mariño had again disobeyed orders and disrupted his plans. Páez advised him to keep Morillo pinned down away from Caracas while Urdaneta took the city, a suggestion that merely goaded Bolívar to cross the Arauca and attack Morillo. His British battalion was led astray by its guides and failed to reach the battleground. Bolívar lost about half of his infantry as well as his desire to drive into Caracas.

Messages now arrived from Santander, who in six months had built up an army in Casanare and had driven off the royalist force Colonel José María Barreiro had brought from New Granada. He reported that the people of New Granada were angered at royalist mistreatment and ready to rebel. Now the prospect of crossing the Andes and liberating New Granada seemed promising. It had many advantages — the royalist army in New Granada would not expect or prepare for such an audacious invasion, and by the time Morillo, who was in winter quarters, learned of it, he could not affect its outcome.

There were also enormous disadvantages, for crossing the country in the rainy season was difficult and hazardous to man and horse. And Bolívar's troops, accustomed only to a tropical climate, would suffer severely from the cold in the mountains. In May, 1819, he called his officers together for a war council in a rude hut on the banks of the Apure. There was no table for maps and papers; the officers sat on the bleached skulls of cattle — a bizarre setting for planning a decisive campaign. Bolívar presented his plan for surprising the royalists in New Granada, while Páez kept Morillo pinned down.

The officers, all young men, listened while Bolívar explained. Since secrecy was vital to success, he announced that they would go by way of Cúcuta, while Santander created a diversion in Casanare to distract the royalists. The troops were not to know their destination, lest some desert and warn the enemy. When he invited his officers to accompany him, only one declined. Colonel James Rooke, the effervescent commander of the British legion, replied, "General, with you I shall go wherever you wish, if necessary down to Cape Horn."

The march began late in May, the troops as usual accompanied by a throng of *juanas,* or camp followers, who nursed the wounded and occasionally even participated in the fighting. To conceal their true destination from potential deserters, Bolívar let it be known they were heading for Cúcuta, although he had ordered Páez to make a diversionary thrust to that region and then fall back to the

Apure. For 120 miles they waded through swamps and across ten navigable rivers, losing many horses and mules and about half of the cattle. Heavy rains kept them drenched much of the time, and when the rains ceased clouds of mosquitos made life miserable. O'Leary commented later, "For seven days we marched in water up to our waists."

Bolívar was always with his troops, eating the same tough beef without salt, sharing all of their discomforts. At Tame Santander met them with two battalions of infantry and two cavalry squadrons, which raised Bolívar's force to around 3,400 men. By mid-June they had reached the foothills of the Andes. To Páez he wrote that "in the face of the new hazards which arise each day and double at every step, I almost despair of ending it. Only constancy which is above every trial, and our determination not to give up a plan that found universal approval, have permitted me to conquer these paths." The worst was not yet over, for the Andes were considered impassable at that season.

For crossing the Andes the troops should have been equipped with leather boots and woolen uniforms, but no such clothing was available in Venezuela. The llaneros were terrified by the awesome heights, and many slipped away. All were cold and miserable, for it rained day and night. It was a crucial test for the army and only Bolívar's unquenchable determination kept the men going. When they complained, he told them that fame and glory awaited them. They struggled on, crossing one crest after another. Many died, and the cavalrymen soon lacked horses.

The last range crossed, the heights of Pisba, was the most difficult of all. The last of the horses died, and to make the difficult ascent the soldiers had to abandon everything but their guns. Rain and icy winds battered the half-naked soldiers, and hundreds died where they fell from exhaustion. Bolívar welcomed the survivors as they straggled out of the mountains. Since the royalists were unaware that a patriot force had crossed the Andes, Bolívar could give his men a few days of rest and reassemble the scattered units. He sent natives to bring in stragglers as well as guns abandoned on the trail. As they gazed back at the foreboding mountains the patriot soldiers knew that they must conquer or perish — retreat was unthinkable.

By this time the scarlet uniforms of the British legion were nothing but rags. On one occasion Bolívar noticed that Colonel Rooke was shirtless, his coat pinned together with thorns. Bolívar ordered his servant to give Rooke one of his own shirts. "How can I, General?" the servant asked. "You have only two shirts. One you are wearing. The other is in the wash."

At the village of Socha the people welcomed the patriots, fed them, and provided horses for the cavalry. They found Colonel Barreiro and the Third Spanish Division blocking the only road from the area; though astonished that the patriots would attempt a campaign in such difficult terrain and during the worst weather, the royalist infantry occupied a rocky hill overlooking the road while 600 cavalrymen waited on the plain. Bolívar rashly ordered an attack, but the royalist position was too strong; it appeared that the patriot army was hopelessly lost. At the crucial moment, however, Bolívar called on Colonel Rooke and the British legion, which charged the royalists with bayonets. "Save the fatherland!" Bolívar called to his llanero cavalry, numbering only 250 men, riding bareback, and armed only with lances. They dashed into the rough terrain, overcoming all obstacles by their skill as horsemen. At dark the fighting ended, with neither side victorious, and both with heavy losses. Bolívar's greatest loss was Colonel Rooke of the British legion.

Although the battle was a standoff, patriot morale remained high while the royalists began to anticipate defeat. "The annihilation of the Republicans appeared inevitable," Barreiro gloomily wrote the viceroy. "Not one seemed able to escape destruction. But despair gave them unequaled courage. Infantry and cavalry rose from the swamps where we had thrown them and began to climb the heights in a real frenzy. . . . Our infantry could not resist them."

Barreiro refused to take further action until he received reinforcements from Bogotá, while Bolívar's activities increased to meet all difficulties and overcome all obstacles. He immediately drafted all able-bodied men into his army, and many Indians offered their services. The patriot army grew by about 800 men, and although few of them had any previous training and the Indians were unaccustomed to using firearms, these men helped win patriot victories.

Early in August Bolívar crossed the Río Sogamoso and drove Barreiro from the village of Paipa. He made elaborate preparations for establishing headquarters and defensive bulwarks to lull the royalists. After dark he ordered his troops to march, avoiding the main road and following trails. The next afternoon he entered Tunja, Barreiro's headquarters, seizing the garrison and arsenal from the 600 royalists who defended it. Bolívar's daring flanking movement, a brilliant maneuver, had completely changed the situation of the two armies, compensated for Bolívar's reckless attack, and decided the outcome of the campaign. The patriots had severed Barreiro's line of communications with Bogotá and blocked his retreat.

Barreiro's main goal now was to escape the trap Bolívar

had skillfully laid for him, which meant abandoning the main road for rough travel through the mountains. Bolívar sent a force to hinder his march and force him to fight. When the battle began in the afternoon of August 7, it was the royalists who were exhausted and out of provisions, and the outnumbered patriots who were well rested and confident. The two armies met as Barreiro approached the bridge of Boyacá, which he had to cross to reach Bogotá.

A detachment of the royalist army crossed the bridge, but the bulk of the army remained nearly a mile away, as if Barreiro had already realized that he could not defeat Bolívar. Santander commanded the patriot troops fighting for possession of the bridge, while Anzoátegui and most of the patriot force was on the mountain slope above the royalists. When the llaneros turned the royalists' right wing and overran the artillery, the battle was over. Sixteen hundred royalists, including Barreiro and his staff, surrendered; all of the royalist munitions also fell to the patriots. The royalists who had escaped were hotly pursued.

Bolívar recognized one of the officers who surrendered — it was Lieutenant Vinoni, who in 1812 had gone over to the royalists and betrayed Bolívar at Puerto Cabello. Bolívar ordered him summarily hanged on the battlefield, as a traitor to his country. He treated the other royalist officers with consideration and courtesy, although most of them feared that they, too, would be hanged or shot, both natives and Spaniards. Most of the troops who surrendered, Granadinos and Spaniards alike, were enlisted in the patriot army.

The way to Bogotá was now open. Viceroy Sámano published a high-flown broadside announcing a great royalist victory, then was frightened out of his wits by news of Barreiro's crushing defeat. Disguising himself as an Indian, he deserted his post and his officials and dashed for the Magdalena. The other royalist officials were quick to follow the viceroy's sagacious example, and fled the city on foot and horseback.

Bolívar entered Bogotá the following day, to the cheers of huge crowds of Granadinos. One, Vicente Azuero, made an impromptu and unwelcome address, praising Bolívar above all heroes of the past in such extravagant terms Bolívar could not stomach it. He preferred, furthermore, to be welcomed by maidens in white. "Great and noble speaker," he interrupted Azuero, "I am not the hero you have painted. Emulate him and I shall admire you." Azuero, his moment on center stage humiliatingly blighted, never forgot nor forgave.

FOUR

From Boyacá to Quito

THE ROYALIST GARRISONS in New Granada concerned Bolívar little and Morillo even less. To the Spanish minister of war Morillo wrote despondently, "As those troops are mostly American, they must by now be increasing the forces of the rebel general." The native royalists were indeed deserting and going over to the patriots, and so Bolívar sent Soublette to Cúcuta to defend the frontier against Morillo and turned his attention to political affairs.

One of his most constant and pressing problems was financing the war, and since New Granada had not been devastated by warfare, he found many sources of money, including 500,000 pesos in the treasury and gold bars worth 100,000 pesos. He established a provisional government with himself as president and Santander as vice-president. He reduced the salaries of civil employees by half, confiscated the property of royalists, made the clergy hand over the tithe to the state treasury, and employed the venerable Spanish practice of requiring "voluntary" contributions from the wealthy.

Santander, himself a Granadino, protested these exactions and urged caution, reminding Bolívar that royal taxes had angered the people more than had the execution of 500 patriots. "Great measures to support an enterprise without resources are indispensable though terrible," Bolívar replied. "Remember the arbitrary means I had to use to achieve the few successes which have saved us. Experience has taught me that one must demand much to get little."

When Bolívar proposed to create new regiments composed of emancipated slaves, Santander protested again. "Is there," Bolívar asked him, "a better or more just way to achieve freedom than to fight for it? Is it just that free men should die to free the slaves? Is it not significant for these bondsmen to win their rights on the battlefield?"

Since royalists still held Cúcuta on the road to Venezuela, as well as Popayán, the Cauca valley, Cartagena, and the highlands between New Granada and Ecuador, it was necessary to establish military control. Bolívar placed officers in charge of all provincial governments. The town governments were not changed, and Spanish taxes remained in effect.

Santander was a logical choice for vice-president, for unlike Bolívar he enjoyed administrative duties. Bolívar once called him the "Man of Laws," but he was actually more concerned with the letter than the spirit of laws, and he had a streak of cruelty, even sadism, in his nature. On occasion he invited prisoners of war to dine with him, thereby giving them hope; then he had them lined up and shot, and appeared to enjoy the grisly sight. On one occasion he exclaimed: "They are bringing me the famous Segovia from Neiva [a captured royalist officer]. I shall celebrate with him in the plaza [which was the usual place of executions]." Although he had many friends and admirers, his own loves were power, money, and self. He was, however, extremely useful to the cause of independence, and Bolívar knew best how to utilize his talents. Though aware of both Santander's covetousness of money and his behind-the-scenes manipulations, Bolívar chose to overlook these shortcomings, as he did with so many of his subordinates.

Writing to Viceroy Sámano, Bolívar offered to exchange Colonel Barreiro and other officers for patriot prisoners. Sámano did not reply. Santander wanted to have all thirty-eight of the royalist officers captured at Boyacá shot, but Bolívar refused, for he was certain that Barreiro, whose fiancée was a Granadina, was ready to join the patriots.

From Angostura came disturbing news that Urdaneta, Arizmendi, and other officers quarreled and plotted, while Zea was proving a poor choice for vice-president. He had unwisely arrested Arizmendi and relieved Mariño of his command, with the result that Mariño came to Angostura and intrigued with congress as well as with Arizmendi's partisans. His attacks were mainly at Zea, but emboldened members of congress began criticizing Bolívar. When news of the victory at Boyacá arrived, for example, they tried to push through a resolution declaring him an outlaw and deserter.

When rumors spread of a royalist army approaching Angostura the congressmen panicked and their attacks on Bolívar grew shrill. Mariño and Arizmendi slyly encouraged the criticism of Bolívar, and meetings of the congress became frenzied. Zea saw that he must resign. The result was that congress elected Arizmendi vice-president and on September 14 brought him triumphantly from prison. He named Mariño commander of the Army of the East and took what he called "vigorous measures," which, as O'Leary explained, meant that they "were directly contradictory to what Bolívar had ordered." Arizmendi was, however, active and effective in raising troops and procuring military supplies.

At the time Arizmendi was taken to Angostura he had quarreled with Urdaneta concerning an expedition to recover Barcelona. Urdaneta, accompanied as usual by his two mistresses, dallied near the royalist garrison at Píritu, waiting for Bermúdez to arrive before attacking. Food became scarce and discipline suffered. Finally Urdaneta reembarked his troops and sailed to Cumaná, where he made a futile attack before marching to Maturín. Bermúdez reached Cumaná too late and was roundly defeated. Urdaneta had no confidence in his British troops, who deserted in disgust at his shooting of prisoners and other atrocities. The senseless campaign was a waste of human and material resources, nothing more.

Before Bolívar left Bogotá the people staged a victory celebration to his liking. Triumphal arches of Roman design were erected as well as six statues depicting the Liberator's virtues. And twenty maidens dressed in white (eight more than in Caracas!) sang a hymn to his glory while placing a crown of laurel on his head. Bolívar took the laurel from his head. "These are the men who deserve it," he said, placing it on Anzoátegui's head, then Santander's, then throwing it to the rifles battalion while the crowd roared its approval. It might be added that one of the white-clad maidens, Bernardina Ibáñez, consoled Bolívar for the loss of Señorita Pepa.

Leaving Santander in charge at Bogotá, Bolívar departed for Angostura on September 20, making a triumphal journey through town after town, collecting money in each. Everywhere he gathered information concerning abuses, and either remedied them on the spot or sent instructions to Santander for action. He wrote Santander advising him to treat General Anzoátegui and his men with the utmost consideration, for they were eager to return to Venezuela. Bolívar was convinced that if these troops left New Granada the royalists would reoccupy it, for "it is impossible for them not to attack again within two months." A few days later, thirty-year-old General Anzoátegui died suddenly, a serious loss to the patriot cause.

A short time later Bolívar wrote Santander that La Torre's force was not worth staying to defeat, but the 1,500 Irish troops of General John Devereux and the divisions of Mariño and Arizmendi were well worth his attention. "Every moment is precious," he said, adding that Zea had advised him to call a congress in New Granada. "We cannot get on with that of Venezuela; what should we do with two?" He warned Santander never to listen to such suggestions. "I am resolved to resign," he concluded, "unless Congress goes into recess for the whole of the coming year. When one is not looking, it votes exactly the law most contrary to the aims I have in mind." A courier from Angostura brought him advice from friends to get there as quickly as possible.

In less than three weeks after Bolívar left Bogotá, Santander had the thirty-eight royalist prisoners shackled and moved from the comfortable quarters Bolívar had provided to a cavalry barracks on the central plaza. There they were informed of Santander's decision to have them shot. Barreiro had fought against the French in the Peninsular campaigns, and though many pleaded for his life, Santander was adamant, claiming he had been conspiring. On horseback he watched the unfortunate prisoners, dragging their heavy shackles, march four abreast across the plaza to be shot in the back. A protestor who boldly reminded him that Bolívar had granted the prisoners a reprieve was also shot. Santander then made a short speech to the multitude, concluding with "I find an inner pleasure in having all *Godos* killed." *Godos,* or Goths, was a contemptuous term for *Peninsulares,* but some of the slain prisoners were in fact Creoles. The executions were to avenge Morillo's killing of patriot leaders earlier. After his speech Santander, preceded by musicians, rode through the main streets singing a song about the executions.

Santander's unnecessary and brutal act drew wide condemnation. Bolívar was outraged, but he did not dare force Santander to resign while La Torre's army was approaching Cúcuta. He recognized it as a serious error, causing a loss of respect for the patriot cause at home and abroad, and he admonished Santander coolly but politely. He continued his journey, sailing down the Apure to the Orinoco with only his staff, arriving unexpectedly in Angostura on December 11. His enemies were totally unprepared for his sudden appearance, for Mariño was with the army and Arizmendi was returning from a visit to Maturín, having sent word that he would reach Angostura on December 11.

On that day Arizmendi was across the river from Angostura. He heard church bells pealing and was pleased at the enthusiastic welcome prepared for him. He sent messengers to confirm his arrival and summon a launch. After waiting a few hours, he sent other messengers. At dark he and his secretary crossed the river in a canoe, his patience worn thin. Shortly after they landed they heard a salvo of artillery, which was also an appropriate form of greeting, but no crowd of well-wishers was there to welcome him. Puzzled, he turned to his secretary. "What can this be?" he asked. Just then both heard shouts of "Viva Bolívar!"

"Adios, General," the secretary said, and quickly disappeared. Only then did Arizmendi realize the bitter truth that his friends had forsaken him.

Bolívar greeted the abashed Arizmendi warmly, concealing his anger at him and the congress, for it was still vital to retain at least the fiction of unity. He did not order an investigation of his enemies' conduct, thereby winning as many friends by policy as he won admirers by military victories. A few days later he reported to the congress on the Boyacá campaign and on his proposed union of Venezuela and New Granada. The new republic should be called "Colombia," he said, to remedy "part of the injustice that has been done to a great man. . . ." Those congressmen who had been loudest in their denunciations of Bolívar were now the most extravagant in their praise and fawning eagerness to please him. They agreed on the union to create the Republic of Gran Colombia and dutifully elected Zea as vice-president of the new republic, Santander as vice-president of Cundinamarca (formerly New Granada) , and Dr. Juan Germán Roscio, "an old, superannuated man enfeebled by debauchery," as vice-president of Venezuela. The third department they planned to incorporate — Quito — was still under royalist control. Bolívar was, of course, elected President of Gran Colombia. Even at this time men suspected him of maneuvering to establish a monarchy with himself as king. A British observer reported that the only reason the republic had not become a kingdom already was the opposition of Páez, Mariño, and a few others. Mariano Montilla, who opposed the union with New Granada, also suspected Bolívar of planning to set up a kingdom for himself, and similar suspicions remained alive for the rest of Bolívar's life.

In Bogotá Santander called an assembly of notables who also approved the union and creation of Gran Colombia, although their vote was unofficial. Bolívar was now anxious to reconcile Creole royalists with the republic, for they were needed as useful citizens. With them in mind he spoke of equal justice to all. "Utmost harshness is needed for all evil-doers," he said, "be they Monarchists or Patriots. . . . Crime is equally hateful in all parties and to be condemned. Let justice triumph and freedom will win." The immediate problem was with the unruly patriot chieftains rather than with royalists. He sent Arizmendi to command the Army of the East, which took care of one troublemaker. Mariño he sent to the Army of the West, confessing to Santander, "I still don't know what to do with this man."

The undercurrent of rivalry and jealousy between Venezuelans and Granadinos was a bitter disappointment to Bolívar. "The misunderstandings which arise out of the union which I tried to establish make me suffer the tortures of the damned," he wrote. "The only reason which prompted me to propose the creation of Gran Colombia was the thought of forever dissipating the causes of hatred, disunity, and disintegration. What a disappointment if these are now multiplying instead."

The problems in dealing with his countrymen were the absence of a spirit of compromise and the lack of a sense of civic responsibility transcending personal ambitions. For the first time an air of pessimism appeared in Bolívar's writings. "I am determined to bid farewell to Venezuela next summer," he wrote in November, "and go to Chile, Buenos Aires, or Lima to die . . . for wherever I go there is disunity and disorder. Soon it will be death. What devilish people we have here!" As his pessimism increased, he wrote later, "I convince myself more and more that neither liberty, nor laws, nor the best instruction, can make us into decent people . . . even less into Republicans or real patriots."

To Bolívar administration was punishment. In order to make any progress toward his major goal he was constantly obliged to overlook and forget acts of enmity and to try to make friends and supporters of foes such as

Mariano Montilla, who had been one of his enemies in Cartagena in 1815. When they met in Angostura in 1819, Bolívar ignored the past and greeted Montilla warmly, asking him to serve on his staff. Greatly relieved, Montilla was completely won over for life. Bolívar named him temporary commander of the Irish legion then on Margarita awaiting the arrival of Devereux. Yellow fever was raging, and 750 members of the legion had already perished.

Although he wished to liberate Caracas and the rest of Venezuela from royalist control, Bolívar had lost his earlier rashness and haste. He left Angostura for the Apure, hoping to use Páez and his llaneros against Morillo. He found their cavalry unfit for hard service because of an epidemic among the horses. By the time they would be ready, he feared, Morillo would have received reinforcements expected from Spain, and the campaign would be too risky. To Santander he wrote, "The enemy must be divided, for divided we can destroy him without risking the fate of Colombia in a general and perhaps fatal battle. Discipline is the soul of these enemy troops just as courage is ours, but it is clear that the former is more useful in battle than mere courage. . . ."

Under the circumstances Bolívar abandoned the Venezuelan offensive in favor of driving the royalists from Cartagena, Maracaibo, and other strongholds. Here the chances of success would be greater and the risks less than in a campaign against Morillo. Before leaving for Bogotá late in December, he sent Zea to Europe as special commissioner to examine claims, consolidate debts incurred by earlier agents, contract a loan, and seek recognition.

On January 1, 1820, Spanish troops awaiting transport to the colonies mutinied under colonels Rafael Riego and Antonio Quiroga, and cowed Ferdinand into restoring the liberal Constitution of 1812. An event of utmost importance for the Spanish-American patriots, this meant that they would have to cope with only the royalist troops already in the Americas, for no more would likely be coming. Although Ferdinand secretly asked France for help, and in 1823 a French army would cross the Pyrenees to restore Ferdinand to absolute rule, it would be too late to affect the outcome of the independence wars.

News of the Riego Revolt reached Spanish America in March, and Morillo subsequently received orders to publish the Constitution of 1812 and to restore peace by "fraternal conciliation." As Morillo knew, however, it would take much more than fraternal conciliation to wipe out the memory of atrocities on both sides. "They have gone crazy in Madrid. . . ." he said in disgust. "Everything is lost. I shall obey, but from now on, one need not count on the subjugation of these provinces." He still had 12,000 troops, about half of them Spaniards, and he still held all of Venezuela except Margarita, Guayana, and the Apure valley, but he had not recovered from his wound, which increased his despondency.

News of the Riego Revolt delighted Bolívar. "What a mad stroke of fate!" he exclaimed. "The news from Spain could not be better. It has decided our fate, for it is now certain that no more troops will come to America. And thus the fight turns in our favor." To Santander he pointed out that "persuaded that she can send no more reinforcements against us, Spain will come to the conclusion that she cannot win and will try to make peace with us to spare herself useless suffering." As an afterthought, he added: "If by accident something were known about a diplomatic negotiation, let wings be put on the post . . . so that the news reaches me flying. I desire that nothing be done without my knowledge in this matter. . . . In matters of peace as in matters of war, it is very important to be a veteran." Assured of ultimate military success, Bolívar turned his attention to diplomatic and political matters, although the troops he had sent toward Ecuador had been thrown back to Popayán.

Reports from Europe were discouraging. Zea had again proved an unfortunate choice, for he foolishly squandered the money obtained, and later turned over the rich Capuchin missions, with 30,000 head of cattle and other valuable assets, to the Englishman Hamilton as part payment of interest on the loan. He also gave Mariño permission to leave for Trinidad. "I forgive him for his disobedience," Bolívar remarked, "but not for the damage done." The missions would have given Bolívar considerable leverage over his mercurial generals, for congress had decreed that confiscated estates were for the benefit of the army, and especially the officers. Of the patriot commanders, only Bolívar and Sucre were not concerned about gaining personal wealth, and holding out the temptation of reward was one of the few effective inducements Bolívar had to keep his subordinates loyal.

Raising money remained a constant problem, yet when Bolívar entered Bogotá in a ragged uniform and without a change of underwear, he signed over his pay to widows and orphans of patriot soldiers because no state funds were available. This was a gesture he made many times during the war.

O'Leary, who became Bolívar's aide after the death of Anzoátegui, and who knew the Liberator well, described his daily routine at this time. He rose at six each morning, dressed, and went immediately to the stables to inspect his horses. Returning to his room he read until nine, breakfasted, and listened to reports of his minister of war and chief of staff. He then read dispatches and petitions, striding back and forth while dictating replies. He answered every letter, but his manner was occasionally abrupt. A physician who had looted some warehouses after Viceroy Sámano fled Bogotá asked to be appointed staff doctor with the rank of lieutenant colonel. Bolívar's reply was blunt: "Be satisfied with what you have stolen." In dictating to his secretaries he expressed his thoughts rapidly, and was annoyed when they could not write fast enough or made errors.

When this daily work was finished Bolívar read until five o'clock. After dinner he went for a ride with his aides, and in the evening talked with officers and friends until nine, when he retired and read until eleven. His favorite authors at this time were Montesquieu and Rousseau, but for leisure reading he preferred history. He frequently sent articles to newspapers, and occasionally wrote verse.

Not all went smoothly in the campaigns of the spring of 1820. Devereux, commander of the Irish legion, left for Jamaica to purchase supplies and failed to return. Montilla sailed with the regiment to Río Hacha in March, but the royalists withdrew to Santa María. Because they were in dire need the Irish troops mutinied when Montilla refused to allow them to sack Río Hacha as compensation for lack of pay. On learning of this disaster, and forgetting both the promises made to the Irish legionaries and their miserable treatment on Margarita, Bolívar wrote Montilla in uncharitable terms. "I am not surprised," he said. "They are like courtesans who do not give themselves before they get their money."

Morillo authorized La Torre to propose an armistice for a month and to indicate that the royalists desired peace. Hoping to create dissension, Morillo also wrote to Páez, Bermúdez, and Montilla concerning the proposed armistice. Páez promptly rebuffed him, referring him to the President of the Republic, to whom he was subordinate. Morillo soon admitted that Bolívar was the key to any negotiations. Neither man was eager to renew hostilities. Bolívar's forces were weak and low on ammunition, but he gave no hint of this in his letters to Morillo.

Among those who defected from the royalists to the patriots at this time was the Indian colonel Juan de los Reyes Vargas, an especially influential leader in western Venezuela. When Morillo marched from Barquisimeto, Reyes Vargas and his guerrillas harassed him constantly, interrupting his communications and capturing stragglers.

Informed that royalist envoys were trying to find his perambulatory headquarters, which changed frequently from Cúcuta to other border towns, Bolívar wrote Morillo that "if these gentlemen's aim is not the recognition of the Republic of Colombia, Y. E. will be good enough to signify to them, from me, that I do not intend to receive them or to listen to any proposal not based on such a principle." He wanted an unequivocal answer within eight days, he added, or he would resume hostilities.

Morillo's reply was that he had no authority to recognize the republic, but he was willing to negotiate with Bolívar as president of a sovereign state. Bolívar nevertheless delayed the negotiations deliberately, in order to conquer Maracaibo, Cartagena, or Santa Marta before the armistice went into effect. He demanded that the royalists evacuate these cities, while mass desertions from the royalist army daily strengthened his bargaining power. Meanwhile royalist garrisons were driven from the Magdalena area and Montilla occupied Santa Marta. At the same time, the patriot commander Valdés was marching toward Quito, and Bolívar retook Mérida and Trujillo.

In an apparent gesture to facilitate negotiations, Bolívar wrote Morillo: "To make our correspondence easier and swifter I shall set my quarters in San Fernando de Apure towards the end of October." To Santander he said, "The aim I had in view was to draw his attention away to San Fernando while our troops operated to the west." He added, "Tell Valdés to be ready to move on Quito as soon as I conceive the idea of an armistice or of an actual peace, so as to gain territory before the order to suspend hostilities reaches him, which order will be conveyed by a Spanish officer who shall proceed slowly owing to the measures we shall take thereto."

Morillo, though he knew the royalist cause was lost, employed similar tactics. "Since hostilities remained open," he wrote, "I did not stop till I had expelled their vanguard from the town of Carache in the neighborhood of Trujillo, with the twofold aim of being ready for decisive action, were we to disagree, and of drawing away from Maracaibo the troops that were attacking it." He sent a messenger to Bolívar suggesting that his retirement to Cúcuta would ease negotiations. Bolívar replied angrily, "Tell him that he will withdraw to Cádiz before I do to Cúcuta," but he agreed to meet Morillo in Santa Ana on November 27.

Morillo, wearing dress uniform and decorations, and accompanied by fifty officers and a squadron of hussars, reached the meeting place first. O'Leary, Bolívar's aide-de-camp, rode into Santa Ana to announce Bolívar's approach. How large an escort has he? Morillo asked. Twelve officers, O'Leary replied. "I thought my bodyguard was small to venture so far forward," Morillo remarked later, "but my old enemy has surpassed me in magnanimity." He sent the hussars back.

When the patriot party approached, Morillo asked which one was Bolívar. "What!" he exclaimed. "That little man in the blue cassock, riding a mule?" O'Leary nodded. Morillo had prepared a banquet, and the two commanders exchanged toasts. They slept that night in the same room. The armistice they drafted began by mentioning the governments of Spain and Colombia, a victory for Bolívar. The rival commanders also agreed concerning the treatment of prisoners and civilians as Bolívar proposed, signing the pact in the same house in Trujillo where Bolívar had endorsed the declaration of the War to the Death. The armistice was for six months, but either side could terminate it on thirty days' notice. Morillo proposed erecting a monument at the site of their meeting, and a huge square stone was placed there to serve as the base for a column which was never placed on it. Soon after this, over the strong protests of his officers, Morillo surrendered his command to La Torre and sailed for Spain, for he knew the royalist cause was irrevocably lost. He had proved his merit as a soldier, but as a statesman he was out of his element, and no rival to Bolívar.

Many patriots criticized the armistice, for unlike Bolívar, who considered it a personal triumph, they failed to see its long-range value. "During the entire course of my public life," Bolívar said,

> I have never revealed more policy or shown more diplomatic ruse than on that important occasion. And in this — I can say it without vanity — I think I surpassed Morillo, as I surpassed him in almost all military operations. I went to the meeting with complete superiority to the Spanish General. I went armed from top to toe with politics and diplomacy, with the semblance of utmost frankness and good will, confidence and friendship. . . . The armistice of six months there concluded, which was so greatly criticized, was for me a mere pretext to let the world see that Colombia negotiated with Spain on an equal footing . . . as power to power.

The armistice, Bolívar continued, was favorable to the patriots but "disastrous for Spain. But there is still more

to be said. The armistice also tricked Morillo into returning to Spain and handing over his command to General
La Torre, who was less able, less active, and less of a
soldier than the Count of Cartagena." Bolívar was thoroughly delighted with what he had achieved. "Never was
a diplomatic comedy played better than that of the day
and night at Santa Ana."

Urdaneta's view was similar. "By treating with the
Spaniards on a footing of equality," he said, "the population of the territories they occupied would see that the
patriots were no longer treated as brigands, but as enemies
worth at least as much as their adversaries."

Bolívar's pleasure at this success was dampened by the
criticism leveled at him by the congress. "The great authorities of Angostura think," he said in contempt, "that
because they are on the Orinoco, they are on the
Thames." They could not see that the patriots needed
the interlude to rebuild their army, for their military
situation had been quite inferior to that of the royalists.

Meanwhile Urdaneta, a native of Maracaibo, was conspiring to oust the royalist officials from the city. His instrument was José María Delgado, a patriot whose three
brothers were royalists. Urdaneta gave him 4,000 pesos to
use in winning over his brothers and other royalists, and
sent a forged order from La Torre that induced most
of the garrison to leave the city.

The ruse worked, and a patriot battalion under Tomás
de Heres quickly occupied the city. When La Torre protested, Urdaneta merely replied that it was lawful to
accept deserters. Bolívar wrote La Torre to apologize for
this violation of the armistice, explaining that Heres
had disobeyed orders, but he shrugged off the return of
Maracaibo to the royalists because of the general opposition to the armistice. Since he had connived in the plot
to seize the city, Bolívar's "regret" was with tongue in

cheek, but his view was that Spain had already lost the war, and the sooner the royalists were driven from the continent the better, and nonviolent methods were preferable to bloodshed. Maracaibo, one of the main royalist bases of operation, was an invaluable prize for the patriots.

The armistice gave Bolívar needed time to improve and enlarge his army, and it also deprived the royalists of Morillo, their ablest general. Although royalists still held Caracas and other Venezuelan cities, Bolívar ordered diversionary attacks by Páez and by Urdaneta, who took Coro in May while Bermúdez struck at Caracas with the Army of the East. Bolívar was no longer concerned over being the first to reenter Caracas, for he dreamed of greater glory to the south once the royalists in Venezuela were defanged. Bermúdez took Barcelona in April, 1821, and entered Caracas in May, only to lose it again to a superior force under Morales.

In June La Torre marched to the plains of Carabobo in what was intended to be a diversionary movement. By this time his mood was defeatist, for desertions had reduced his army to 5,000 men, while Bolívar's had grown to 6,500. Bolívar divided the patriot army into three columns under Páez, Cedeño, and Ambrosio Plaza, with Mariño as adjutant general. Royalist artillery covered the valley Bolívar would have to follow to reach the plains, which were surrounded by hills. Bolívar sent Páez by a little-known trail to strike the enemy on flank and rear while the main force assaulted the enemy center. Páez ordered an untimely charge and found himself caught in terrain difficult for cavalry and exposed to heavy fire.

The British legion advanced on the royalist main force and drew the enemy fire, losing seventeen officers in almost as many minutes, but allowing Páez to recover. As the British legion and the Apure battalion overran royalist positions and pushed the enemy onto the plains with fixed bayonets, Páez and his llaneros made a devastating charge. The royalists broke and ran, with the lancers in hot pursuit.

During the heat of battle Páez saw his bodyguard, El Negro Primero, leave the fray and ride to the rear. Thinking El Negro Primero had lost his courage, Páez angrily asked him if he was afraid and ordered him to go back and get himself killed. "No, my General," El Negro Primero replied, "I came to bid you farewell. General, I can't go back to get myself killed, because I'm already dead." Lifeless, he slid from his horse.

With only one regiment, La Torre and Morales fled through Valencia to Puerto Cabello. The royalist garrison at La Guaira tried to join them, but was forced to surrender. Only Puerto Cabello and Cumaná remained in royalist control, but some scattered units had escaped destruction at Carabobo. And although Coro had fallen to the patriots, the people remained stubbornly royalist and recovered the city from their liberators. The battle of Carabobo was costly for the patriots, for they lost many able officers, including Cedeño and Plaza. The day after the battle Bolívar wrote Santander that "yesterday a splendid victory confirmed the political birth of the Republic of Colombia." He called the army "the greatest and finest ever to bear arms on any battlefield in Colombia."

When Bolívar entered Caracas the city was virtually deserted, and no white-gowned maidens awaited him with songs and laurel wreaths. He found most of his houses and estates in ruins. He reorganized the government along republican forms but actually under military rule. Páez, Bolívar knew, would rule Venezuela, though he was ill-prepared for the task and, from Bolívar's viewpoint, was

undependable. To counteract him Bolívar named Soublette as vice-president, but since Páez remained commander of the army, in any dispute his was the deciding
vote.

The law calling for the expropriation of the property
of émigré royalists was immediately invoked, but to
soften the effects of the harsh measure Soublette ordered
the confiscated estates administered by heirs or relatives
of the émigrés. Bolívar, who was in a less forgiving mood,
revoked the order. He did, however, ask congress to return to Francisco Iturbe his sequestered property, for he
had not forgotten Iturbe's generosity in securing a pass
for him from Monteverde in 1812. Congress complied
with this request.

The Riego Revolt of 1820 had resulted in the freeing of
Antonio Nariño, and the Granadino statesman had returned to New Granada in time to preside over a meeting
of the national assembly at Cúcuta in May, 1821. At this
meeting the union of Venezuela and New Granada was
unanimously approved. Nariño was Bolívar's choice for
vice-president of New Granada, but owing to ill health
as well as to strong opposition, he resigned.

Bolívar informed the assemblage at Cúcuta that he
would not accept the presidency. "I am tired . . . of ruling this Republic of ingrates," he said. "I am tired of being called a usurper, tyrant, and despot. . . ." The congress, to no one's surprise, refused to accept his resignation
and appealed to his patriotism. To friends in Cúcuta
Bolívar wrote a warning that indicated he was well aware
of his own inner feelings and had a clear view of the
future: "It is not advisable that the commander in chief
of the army should administer justice, for a general conflict is sure to rise against this individual, and when he
falls the whole government will fall."

Venezuela was chaotic, devastated, exhausted, and Bolívar was anxious to leave it and launch his campaign to liberate Quito. "Nothing can be done," he wrote of Venezuela, "because the good people have disappeared and the bad ones have multiplied."

The congress in Cúcuta continued to maintain that Bolívar must serve as president. He went there in September, insisting that he was incapable of ruling the republic. If, however, the congress insisted, he would accept for the duration of the war, but only on condition that he be permitted to complete the campaign in the south.

The Constitution of Cúcuta that the assembly produced was liberal in tone, giving the legislature supremacy over the president, who had little power except in wartime. Bolívar saw little merit in it, for he was thoroughly accustomed to making the decisions and giving orders, and he did not intend to be frustrated by a gaggle of quarrelsome congressmen. The constitution-writers envisaged the addition of Ecuador to the union, and for this reason agreed that the capital of Gran Colombia should be at Bogotá, a decision that angered Venezuelans.

Although the constitution-writers were presumably of liberal persuasion and regarded Bolívar as conservative, he proposed that the children of slaves be freed, for he knew that the large landowners would react violently to any attempt to free all slaves. Bolívar made the request as a personal reward for the victory at Carabobo, and the congress could not refuse. The Indian tribute, or head tax, was also abolished, but it continued to be collected for some years, just as some of the sons of slaves continued in bondage.

The Constitution of Cúcuta contained, in Bolívar's view, fatal flaws that doomed it to failure, for under it men still considered themselves Venezuelans or Granadinos rather than citizens of Gran Colombia. The constitution was, in other respects, not vastly different from that of Angostura.

A special law of congress authorized Bolívar to continue his military campaigns against the royalists, and provided for the vice-president to administer the government in his absence. Bolívar suggested Santander for the post of vice-president, though he would still have preferred Nariño. Santander was duly elected.

Far from satisfied with the arrangements made, Bolívar was apprehensive of the future. Concerning the military leaders upon whom he had to depend, such as Páez, Bermúdez, and Mariño, he wrote, "We find ourselves at the edge of an abyss, or rather on top of a volcano that may soon erupt. I fear peace more than war." To the vice-president, he said, "Does it not seem to you, my dear Santander, that these legislators who are more ignorant than evil and more presumptuous than ambitious, will lead us into anarchy and tyranny and finally to destruction? If it is not the llaneros who will bring about our ruin, then it will be the gentle philosophers of Colombia." Although the Granadinos were urbane and cultured, while the llaneros were crude savages, Bolívar did not delude himself into thinking the former were more reliable. For this reason he would accept the title of president to facilitate obtaining funds for his military campaigns, leaving the onerous and unrewarding tasks of administration to others. Santander relished the administrative routine and especially the power of office that Bolívar found so distasteful.

Royalists still held Cartagena, the strongest fortified city in South America. Bolívar sent Colonel Mariano Montilla to besiege it, in conjunction with Admiral José Padilla and aided by Colonel Friedrich de Adlercreutz, a Swedish soldier of fortune, whose feigned attack enabled

Padilla to enter the bay and capture eleven royalist vessels. Montilla offered honorable surrender terms to royalist General Gabriel Torres. Because the city was now cut off from aid by land or sea Torres accepted them on October 1. Two weeks later Cumaná surrendered to Bermúdez, who sent the royalist garrison to Puerto Rico in Colombian ships.

It is almost surprising that Bolívar, with such a prophetic view of the future, continued the exhausting struggle for Spanish-American independence. "Neither you nor I shall, in our old age," he prophesied to Santander, "see that sincere harmony which should exist in the big family of a state." The forces of disintegration and disharmony were too powerful to allow unity to exist. But as long as he could satisfy his insatiable craving for glory at the head of an army, Bolívar could not stop. Bogotá, the former seat of a viceroyalty, had made him forget the provincial capital of the captaincy-general of Venezuela. Lima, "The City of Kings" and one-time capital of most of the continent, beckoned. Santander could rule Gran Colombia while Bolívar won honor, glory, and adulation in the south. And perhaps his name would make possible the ultimate union of all of Spanish America. Even in the face of the coldest facts, Bolívar could dream impossible dreams. He turned his attention to Quito, which was still royalist, although the port city of Guayaquil had declared for independence in 1820.

Argentine General José de San Martín, who had liberated Chile in 1817–18, had landed on the coast of Peru with his Army of the Andes in 1820. There San Martín had refused to risk the fate of Peru on the outcome of a single battle, and had allowed the royalists to withdraw from Lima into stronger positions in the mountains without any attempt to force them to surrender. The royalists, owing to San Martín's inactivity, now gained strength

even though the Riego Revolt ended any hope that reinforcements would arrive from Spain. Despite the royalist
threat San Martín and Peruvian officers were eager to add
Guayaquil and Quito to Peru. Bolívar intended to thwart
those hopes.

To reach Quito by land it was necessary to pass through
the fanatically royalist town of Pasto by a difficult mountain route. The people of Pasto were not only uncompro-
misingly loyal to Ferdinand — they also occupied positions
from which it was almost impossible to dislodge them. In
1820 the patriot force Bolívar had sent under Antonio
Obando had been surprised and annihilated in Popayán
because the people deceived him concerning the approach
of royalist forces from Pasto. Although patriots under
Valdés had reconquered Popayán, the fierce Pasteño resistance had not been overcome. The Pasteños were led by
Bishop Salvador Ximénez of Popayán, who in Spain had
fought as a guerrilla warrior against the French.

In January, 1821, Bolívar sent Sucre, his most trusted
and capable lieutenant, to replace Valdés and to continue
the campaign into Ecuador. Sucre rebuilt the tattered
army, but soon found there was little chance of fighting
his way through Pasto without heavy losses. Wisely sparing
his army such unnecessary hardships, he marched to Buenaventura on the Pacific coast, secured ships, and sailed to
Guayaquil with his troops.

Santander, who wanted to shoot all of the Pasteño leaders and ship all of the men far away, sent General Pedro
León Torres with a patriot force against Pasto. Torres and
his troops were so badly mauled they even abandoned
Popayán to the royalists, leaving Sucre in Guayaquil with
only 300 men. To help strengthen Sucre's position Bolívar
wrote the poet José Joaquín Olmedo, president of the
Guayaquil junta, "I am pleased to believe, Most Excellent
Sir, that the Republic of Colombia shall be proclaimed in

that capital before my entrance therein. Your Excellency must know that Guayaquil is part of Colombian territory." This was not exactly true, for although colonial Quito had been subordinate to the viceroy of New Granada, Guayaquil had been administered by Peru, and many Guayaquilians favored Peru over Gran Colombia.

Early in 1822, even before he had any marked success in the south, Bolívar was thinking beyond the upcoming campaign to matters of continental scope. He wrote to Chilean liberator Bernardo O'Higgins and to General San Martín in Lima to introduce the concept of a confederation of states. At the same time he sent Miguel Santamaría to Mexico and Joaquín Mosquera to Peru, Chile, and Argentina in his eagerness to make his vision of a Spanish-American league a reality. It occurred to Bolívar that, because of Spanish-American intransigence, he might have to impose his ideas on some of the countries by military force, but that idea was more appealing than disheartening. Napoleon was still his idol, and he still found Napoleon's methods acceptable, even preferable. Because he believed firmly that he was destined to create a federation of Spanish-American states, he felt that the ways and means were of secondary importance. And, as he often said, war was his element.

While concluding preparations for his triumphal move southward, he warned Santander: "Be careful, my friend, that you have four to five thousand men for me, so that Peru yields me two victories like Boyacá, Carabobo. I do not wish to lose the fruits of eleven years through one defeat, and I do not wish San Martín to see me other than I deserve to be seen, namely as the chosen son."

At first Bolívar planned to go to Panama and take ship to Guayaquil, but he feared that San Martín might annex Guayaquil to Peru before he could attach it to Gran Colombia. By the time he sent General Montilla to Panama, the Panamanians had declared their independence and had indicated a desire to unite with Gran Colombia. As a result, he sent Sucre directly to Guayaquil.

Antonio José Sucre de Alcalá, an aristocrat from Cumaná, was of Flemish descent. He was well known for his courage in battle; Bolívar called him the "best general of the Republic and its first statesman." When O'Leary first saw Sucre approach on horseback, he asked Bolívar who the poor rider was. "He is one of the best officers in the army," Bolívar replied. "Strange as it may seem, he is not well known, nor does anyone suspect his capabilities. I am determined to bring him out of obscurity, for I am convinced that some day he will rival me." As the only one who thoroughly understood and appreciated Bolívar's continental ideas, it was logical that Bolívar should consider Sucre his proper successor. He loved Sucre as if he had been his own son, and Sucre reciprocated fully. But as Sucre's star rose, it was no easy task for Bolívar to conquer his envy and jealousy. If Sucre had been less modest and self-effacing, if he had not been devoid of theatrical gestures, and if he had been less devoted to Bolívar, it does not seem likely that Bolívar could have considered him other than as a rival for "glory."

Before heading south Bolívar ordered various units to assemble in Popayán. Some had to march great distances to reach the city and lost one-third of their men along the way. Many more died after reaching it, for during the war many thousands more men were lost to disease and exposure than to enemy bullets. New Granada alone had sent 20,000 recruits to form the army that numbered only 6,000 when it entered the plains of Carabobo to meet the enemy. In four years the rifles battalion had received 22,000 replacements, yet it numbered only 600 men by the time it reached Quito. Although desertions accounted for a large part of the losses, the rifles battalion was, under

Colonel Arthur Sandes, one of the best-disciplined units of the whole army, and its desertions were minimal.

Sucre's difficult mission in Ecuador was to suppress royalist attempts to recover Guayaquil, to aid the patriots there to overthrow the royalist regime in Quito, and to annex all of Ecuador to Gran Colombia. In 1820 the Guayaquil patriots had marched over the mountains to Quito, where royalist Governor Melchor Aymerich had destroyed their force. Sucre eventually had about 1,000 men, not enough to assail the almost impregnable royalist position in Quito. He was faced, too, with the fact that annexation to Gran Colombia was unpopular, for many people still favored union with Peru.

The patriots of Guayaquil, knowing that they lacked strength to prevent a royalist reconquest, gladly accepted the help Bolívar had sent them. Sucre's force, combined with that of Guayaquil, was still too weak and too ill-equipped for the difficult ascent and assault on Quito. While they were pondering this problem Governor Aymerich sent two royalist divisions of 3,000 men to reconquer Guayaquil. With fewer than 1,500 men Sucre defeated one division and drove off the other. He tried to follow up his victory by pursuing and scattering the royalists, but the mountain terrain made this a costly and futile effort.

The royalists of Quito were reinforced late in 1821 when General Juan de la Cruz Mourgeon arrived with 1,000 men. At about the same time Bolívar began his march south, planning to sail from Buenaventura or to force his way through the mountains to Quito. After learning that Spanish warships were cruising off the Pacific coast, he had given up the thought of going by sea. The people of Pasto still blocked the only trail between Popayán and Quito, and their royalist fervor was in no way diminished. Anxious to avoid a costly fight with them, Bolívar tried various subterfuges, such as the distribution of fake documents and newspaper accounts to convince them that further resistance was hopeless.

The royalist commander at Pasto, Basílio García, knew that his defensive position could be held indefinitely by a few determined men, and he had no intention of compromising. García was hated by many of his officers for his cruelty, and but for Valdés's execution of prominent royalists in Popayán, some would have gone over to the patriots. The difficult, exhausting travel, together with the extreme cold of the mountains, formed part of the royalist defense. Bolívar began the march with 3,000 men, but 30 men had fallen ill each day. Royalist guerrillas drove off the cattle and burned the farms along the way, while others harassed Bolívar's rear guard, adding hunger to the troops' woes. By the time he neared Pasto his force had been reduced to 2,000 men.

The royalist army of 1,800 men awaited the patriots in the hills above the crossing of the Guáitara. Bolívar rashly attempted to force a crossing by sending Valdés into the rocky hills to turn the royalist left wing, while General Pedro Torres attacked the royalist center with the main force. Patriot losses were shockingly high — Torres and other high-ranking officers received fatal wounds trying to do the impossible for Bolívar. "How well my people go into battle," Bolívar remarked proudly as his troops courageously assaulted the heights. "Yes," was the reply, "but they do not return."

The battle of Bombona, as it was called, was one of the costliest of the wars. When Bolívar saw that his troops had encircled the royalists, he threw reserves against the enemy center, and by the time darkness ended the fighting the royalists had given way, though neither side could claim a victory. As Obando remarked, "Both sides lost the battle; we, our force; the Spaniards, the battlefield." Because

he could not leave his wounded to be slaughtered by guerrillas, Bolívar made no effort to pursue the retreating Pasteños. He was much depressed, for he had sacrificed one-
third of his army.

In the morning the royalist commander sent Bolívar
two Colombian flags his men had captured, for, he said,
he did not want trophies from an enemy he could destroy
but not conquer. He suggested that Bolívar withdraw to
Popayán, but Bolívar opened negotiations with him in an
effort to gain time until reinforcements arrived. He was
severely criticized for the costly effort to do the impossible.
His attack did, however, prevent the Pasteños from joining the royalist garrison in Quito against Sucre. When
reinforcements arrived Bolívar continued the march, although he was so ill he had to be carried in a litter. He
offered generous surrender terms, but it was difficult for
García to persuade the Pasteños to negotiate, and it required the aid of the bishop to convince them. Bolívar
appointed negotiators and continued on to Pasto with
only his aides, hoping by this hazardous display of confidence in his foes to allay their mistrust.

Sucre's army was reinforced by about 1,000 Argentine
and Peruvian troops San Martín had sent in hope of at-
taching Ecuador, or at least Guayaquil, to Quito. When
San Martín had landed in Peru the royalist Numancia
battalion, composed of Granadinos, had gone over to him
and Sucre had asked for this battalion. Instead San Martín sent the troops under Andrés Santa Cruz that were stationed in Piura, and they met Sucre and his army south of
Quito. On the way to Quito they were joined by the rem-
nants of an 800-man force sent from Panama, which had
lost two-thirds of its complement on the march from
Guayaquil through the mountains.

Aymerich and the royalist garrison of Quito prepared
defenses to the south, expecting Sucre to strike from that

direction. Instead he slipped past the royalist right flank undetected and scaled the heights of the volcano of Pichincha before dawn on May 24. When they discovered him, the royalists rashly attacked, and in the battle of Pichincha Sucre won as thorough a victory as Bolívar had gained at Boyacá. General Aymerich surrendered and Quito fell — Ecuador was now in patriot control. The people of the city, who were staunchly propatriot, had kept Sucre informed of royalist activities during his march, and welcomed him as their deliverer.

Bolívar, who had yearned for the glory of liberating Quito, but who had been prevented by the stubborn Pasteño resistance, could not conceal his envy of Sucre. "You must understand that it was by my request that García surrendered," he wrote Santander,

> for no one there knew anything about Sucre's battle, nor could we have known. For this reason I do not want Sucre to be given credit for García's capitulation. In the first place Sucre has had enough fame; secondly, it is true, very true, that the capitulation had been decided upon without knowledge of Sucre's activities. It seems to me that it would be proper to write something about this in the State papers in which both deeds are recorded. Sucre had a larger number of troops and a smaller number of enemies. . . . I believe that with a little tact one could honor my division very greatly without detracting from Sucre's.

Bolívar soon overcame the twinge of jealousy of Sucre, his ablest subordinate and his most devoted and trusted friend. Much of the patriot success was the product of his skill and sacrifice, which Bolívar freely admitted. Sucre always gave Bolívar frank and excellent advice, but he was not popular and had no large following outside of the army.

Bolívar's immediate goals were to subordinate or exterminate the Pasteños so they could not cut communications between Quito and Bogotá, to bring Quito into Gran Colombia, and to negotiate with San Martín over Guayaquil. The bishop of Popayán, who had inspired Pasteño resistance, now offered to resign and depart. Bolívar tactfully replied that he could not allow him to abandon his people — his duty was to remain with his flock until the Holy See recognized Gran Colombia as an independent state. By such discreet and tactful treatment Bolívar won over the bishop as he had other enemies.

Winning over the Pasteños, however, was far less successful, for although they were outwardly submissive, they watched for opportunities to rebel and kill patriot troops and officers. A nephew of the former llanero leader, Benito Boves, fled to Pasto after Pichincha and incited a rebellion. Bolívar sent Sucre with 2,000 men, but he was unable to dislodge Boves from Taindala. With reinforcements commanded by British colonel Thomas Charles James Wright, Sucre took Taindala. The Pasteños stubbornly refused to surrender but were defeated after hard and bloody fighting. Because of the fanatic resistance the patriots were not generous in victory, and, according to O'Leary, "in the horrible massacre that ensued, soldiers and civilians, men and women, were sacrificed promiscuously" in the three days of uncontrolled vengeance. Later Bolívar himself went to Pasto and repaid the Pasteños for his humiliating defeat. He ordered all estates confiscated and given to his officers, then conscripted all men who had served in the army and sent them away. He left Bartolomé Salom in command with instructions to arrest and send to Quito or Guayaquil any man who had escaped conscription. Many Pasteños committed suicide.

After Sucre's victory at Pichincha and the Pasteños' capitulation Bolívar had proceeded slowly to Quito, where he arrived in mid-June. His reception was quite different from that in Pasto, for everyone from lowest to highest welcomed him with wild enthusiasm, and he was in his element. He warmly embraced Sucre, and together they rode through the city streets while maidens vied for the opportunity to crown them with laurel wreaths. One young lady did so in an unconventional but effective manner, for as Bolívar rode beneath a balcony a wreath sailed through the air and bounced off his head. He looked up in surprise to see the attractive face of Manuela Sáenz de Thorne, wife of an English physician in Lima. That same night at a ball in Bolívar's honor, he met Manuela, and long before the dancing had ended the two had slipped away.

Manuela opened a new chapter in Bolívar's life, for his liaison with her was permanent, quite unlike the temporary unions with his other mistresses, not to mention his countless one-night affairs. She would remain with or near him for the remaining decade of his life. She did not, however, replace all other women in his life. She was simply added to them, a physical strain that even Bolívar's robust constitution could not endure.

The illegitimate daughter of a Spaniard, Manuela had been educated in a convent in her native Quito. Convent life was martyrdom to the high-spirited and uncontrollable girl, who was accustomed to being the center of attraction. She was allowed to visit her mother once a month, and on one of these visits ran off with a young Spanish officer, who apparently deserted her. Her family returned her to the convent, but soon married her to James Thorne, who was twenty years her senior. Although her marriage to Thorne gave her a position in society and opportunities for the sort of life she desired, she felt no strong attachment to him.

Dr. Thorne moved to Lima, where Manuela watched

San Martín's Army of the Andes enter the city after the royalists had withdrawn. The ladies of Lima were thrilled at the opportunities for political intrigue, and their salons were the locales of political movements. Rosita Cámpazano, like Manuela an Ecuadorian, became San Martín's mistress, and she and Manuela were friends.

Manuela had returned to Quito for a visit with relatives, arriving on the day of Sucre's triumph at Pichincha, and she was there when Bolívar arrived in triumph. Theirs was a tempestuous love affair that caused many tongues to wag — gossips called her a nymphomaniac, but this was not the worst thing said of her. After joining Bolívar she shocked conventional people by wearing a cavalry colonel's uniform and dashing about with a cavalry escort, oblivious to her husband's pleas to return to him. But she was thoroughly devoted to Bolívar, and would not only gather intelligence information for him in Lima, but one day would save his life.

FIVE

The Road to Ayacucho

BOTH GRAN COLOMBIA and Peru wanted to annex Ecuador, and troops from both countries took part in the victory at Pichincha. Fearing separatist movements in Ecuador, Bolívar created a department of the country and, over Sucre's protests, named him president. On learning that Guayaquil was ready to accept the Constitution of Gran Colombia, Bolívar sent troops there to forestall San Martín, and went there himself in July. He had prudently left the Peruvian-Argentine troops in Quito, sending only Colombians to Guayaquil. Seeing themselves outmaneuvered, and knowing that there was a pro-Peru party in Guayaquil, the Peruvians suggested that the city itself should decide on its destiny. Bolívar merely agreed to ask the people their views.

There was in Guayaquil more confusion than consensus, for three groups were vying for power — those who favored Gran Colombia, those who preferred Peru, and those who wished to be independent of both. Adding to the tensions were rumors that a Peruvian naval squadron was on its way. The cabildo of Guayaquil tried to retain its freedom of action, but Bolívar quickly convinced the councillors that he would make the major decisions. To the people he pictured himself as their savior: "You find yourselves in a false and ambiguous position," he told them. "You are threatened with anarchy. I bring you salvation." He was convinced, he told them, that they wanted to be Colombians, but he promised to let them vote for incorporation, so the world would know that every Colombian loved his country.

The tensions increased as crowds thronged the streets and threatened life and property. While the cabildo members sought safety in flight, Bolívar publicly frowned on the rioting while secretly encouraging it. When conditions became sufficiently turbulent, the cabildo would have no choice but to invite him to assume civil as well as military power, for any people of property preferred the rule of one man to anarchy. Meanwhile he solemnly maintained that he would not interfere with the people's freedoms.

San Martín requested a meeting with Bolívar to discuss the fate of Guayaquil, but Bolívar was slow to respond. After liberating Chile San Martín had landed on the Peruvian coast with 4,500 men soon after the Riego Revolt in 1820. He had conferred with Viceroy Joaquín de la Pezuela, demanding Peru's independence under a constitutional monarchy and a European prince. Other royal officials, determined not to compromise, had deposed Pezuela and named General José de la Serna viceroy. La Serna had withdrawn his army from Lima and marched into the sierra unmolested; San Martin entered the capital in July, 1821.

Proclaiming himself "Protector of Peru," San Martín had appointed mainly Argentines to his cabinet. He failed to launch an aggressive campaign against the royalists, with the result that many of his troops and Peruvian recruits went over to the enemy in disgust at the inactivity. Confidence in San Martín declined seriously, and it became clear that Peru would need additional outside aid to make the independence San Martín had proclaimed a reality. Assuming that Bolívar was still in Quito, in July, 1822, San Martín sailed for Guayaquil, planning to annex the port city and province to Peru before conferring with Bolívar in Quito.

When San Martín reached Guayaquil it was too late, for Bolívar had skillfully outmaneuvered him, and he found that he had absolutely no bargaining power. Bolívar held the upper hand on every issue, and San Martín was reduced to asking for military help. Bolívar offered to send four battalions, less than 2,000 men, obviously an insufficient force. San Martín pointed out that Peruvian independence would require the entire Colombian army commanded by Bolívar himself. This was impossible, Bolívar told him, for royalists still held Puerto Cabello. San Martín's offer to serve under Bolívar was also rejected.

The two men conferred privately on board the Peruvian warship *Macedonia,* and since no record was made of their conversations the meeting has inspired endless speculation by partisans of both great leaders. On his return to Peru San Martín admitted to his staff that "the Liberator had anticipated us." Later he added the cryptic remark, "The Liberator is not the man we imagined him to be." While San Martín was in Guayaquil there had been an uprising against his hated minister Bernardo Monteagudo.

San Martín remained in Peru only a month after his return. "I am tired of being called a tyrant . . . of having people say that I want to be King, Emperor, or even the devil," he said. He resigned and left the country. Later he made the bitter comment, "The attempts of twenty-four years to promote liberty have produced no more than calamities. . . . Liberty! Give a child of two years a box of razors to play with and see what will happen!"

Bolívar waited for Peruvians to realize how desperately they needed his help, for he did not intend to make a move until they were willing to concede the powers he would need. Publicly he gave the appearance of having completely satisfied his ambitions. "Now all I need," he said, "is to bring my treasure to safety and to hide it in a deep cavern, so that no one can steal it. In other words, all I need now is to retire and to die. By God, I wish for nothing more. It is the first time that I have been satisfied with my lot." This was, however, for Peruvian consumption, for he still had a burning desire to be the liberator of Peru.

Inwardly, Bolívar dreamed not only of the glory of freeing Peru but of creating a league of Spanish-American states from Mexico to Argentina. Santander urged him to return to Bogotá in order to exert pressure on the congress, and there were also requests that he return to Venezuela. When Santander remarked that now everything had to be done according to the letter of the constitution, Bolívar was deeply offended, for he had grown quite accustomed to exercising dictatorial powers and he was not prepared to govern any other way. He did not appreciate Santander's unsubtle reminder.

"I shall not keep the presidency if I am not given those extraordinary powers which Congress has voted me," he replied. "I am convinced that Colombia can only be kept in order and well-being by absolute power. Colombia needs an army of occupation which will keep it free."

San Martín's resignation left Peru in a state of near-anarchy and threatened by a royalist army. Bolívar wrote offering his services, but the triumvirate named by the congress to run the government was willing to accept only Colombian arms, not troops. The Colombian troops Bolí-

var had sent to Lima at San Martín's request met such un-
concealed animosity their commander returned with them
to Guayaquil.

In Guayaquil a group Bolívar had called together engaged in heated debate until he sent word that he wished
the meeting to end, since its only purpose was to declare
the province annexed to Gran Colombia. The assembly
voted for annexation and adjourned. Members of the
junta and others left for Peru, where they were given official positions as well as the opportunity to assuage their
wounded pride by increasing Peruvian hostility toward
Bolívar and the Colombians.

In January, 1823, the royalists of Peru defeated the
army under General Andrés Santa Cruz so thoroughly that
only 500 of the 4,000 men escaped. After this crushing defeat the Peruvian garrison in Lima forced the junta to
resign, and José de la Riva-Agüero was named president.
In February he sent an agent to Bolívar, asking for a new
army to liberate Peru. By this time Bolívar was considering leaving the Peruvians to their fate. "The clamorers
want new and weak governments," he wrote, "which will
make revolutions and still more revolutions. Not I. I do
not want a weak government. I would rather die on the
ruins of Colombia fighting for its principles and its unity."

In April, a few days after Riva-Agüero had pleaded with
him to come to Peru and take command, Bolívar learned
that royalist commander Morales had launched a campaign to take Mérida and Trujillo in Venezuela. He immediately started north, but soon received word that
Morales had withdrawn, and so returned to Guayaquil.
Each week he received ever more urgent requests from
Peru. He wrote Santander that "nothing less than a mag-
nificent army, with a very strong government and a
Caesarian man, can wrench Potosí and Cuzco from the
Spaniards." At the same time the captain of the Peruvian

transports assured him that unless he went to Peru to take command there was no point in sending troops.

"Lima lives today like a dead body animated by vital spirits," Bolívar wrote. It was "the hope of my coming that has revitalized that dead body. No one dreams, no one thinks, no one imagines that Peru can exist without me." At the same time he had doubts. "I fear that my coming to Lima may be looked upon with much suspicion by my enemies. . . . The desire to end war in America drives me to Peru, but I am thrown back by love of my reputation, so that I hesitate and decide nothing." Throughout his life Bolívar suffered deeply from unjust criticisms and calumnies.

Although the people of Pasto had been brutally repressed and punished for their fanatical royalism, a number of Pasteños had hidden in the woods, awaiting an opportunity to strike. In June, when they noticed that many of the troops had been withdrawn, they armed themselves with sticks, spears, or any weapons they could find. Led by Agustín Agualongo, an astute and courageous Indian, they attacked the garrison so fiercely the patriots were overpowered. Bolívar himself took charge of the troops sent against them. "The infamous Pasto has again raised her hateful seditious head," he wrote, "but this head shall be cut off forever. . . . This shall be the last time in the life of Pasto. . . ."

Bolívar rounded up all available men, including convalescents in the hospitals and local militia, and with 2,000 of them routed Agualongo's horde at Ibarra, killing 800, showing no quarter, taking no prisoners. Agualongo escaped into the mountains, where he wisely rejected an offer of amnesty. Colonel Salom occupied Pasto unopposed, under orders from Bolívar that meant virtual extermination of the population and replacing it with outsiders. No metal was allowed in the region. All men who immediately came forward and surrendered were shipped to Guayaquil. Others were to be shot on sight. Salom carried out these Assyrian terms so savagely that he was again threatened by Agualongo and 1,500 desperate Pasteños.

Salom defeated the Pasteños, but they regrouped and threatened him again, for they had nothing to lose. Salom wrote Bolívar that halfway measures were not enough — he should either issue a general pardon or give orders for total annihilation, which was the course Salom preferred. "No idea can be conveyed of the obstinate tenacity and resentment of the Pasteños: if heretofore it is the majority of the population that has declared war against us, now it is the total mass of them that wages war against us with a fury I cannot express," he wrote Bolívar. Pasto remained in a state of rebellion for about a year before the people were ground down.

While Bolívar was involved with the Pasteño rebellion the situation in Peru changed, for Sucre refused to assume command of the allied army in order to force the Peruvians to accept Bolívar. Royalist General José de Canterac marched to the coast with 7,000 men, and the Peruvian war council ordered Lima evacuated. Canterac entered the city in June, and by threatening to burn it, extracted huge sums from the population. The Peruvian congress met in Callao and voted to send another delegation to Bolívar and to grant Sucre dictatorial powers in the interim. Congress also deposed Riva-Agüero, who countered by dissolving congress, which named the Marqués de Torre Tagle president. Canterac, learning that Santa Cruz was marching into the sierra, plundered Lima and abandoned it in July. In desperation Peruvian officers sent an agent to Chile to invite San Martín to return, but he politely declined.

In a pact with Peru Bolívar agreed to send 6,000 men

and soon had two divisions of 2,000 men each on their way. Peru insisted that Bolívar come to take command. He requested permission from the Congress of Gran Colombia. While waiting for a reply he named General Manuel Valdés to command the Colombian divisions, but sent Sucre to Lima as minister plenipotentiary, with ample authority to intercede in military affairs. He warned both Sucre and Riva-Agüero, however, that there were to be no military actions without him.

Early in August, 1823, Bolívar received the permission requested of congress and sailed for Peru. He warned the delegation of Peruvians who welcomed him, "You may count on me only if you do away with the malpractices and institute reforms in all branches of the government where venality and decadence appear." Torre Tagle and others found this warning ominous.

"Peruvian affairs have reached a peak of anarchy," Bolívar wrote. "Only the enemy army is well organized, united, strong, energetic, and capable. The Patriot army is lost. Seven warlike powers fight one another under the flags of Peru, Chile, Colombia, Buenos Aires, the Government, Parliament, and Guayaquil." The situation appeared so hopeless Bolívar knew that he was risking his reputation by accepting command. "I shall always be the foreigner to most people," he said despondently, "and I shall always arouse jealousies and distrust in these gentlemen. . . . I have already regretted that I came here."

Sucre echoed these fears. "I don't know whether I may congratulate myself on his Excellency's arrival in Peru," he told Bolívar. "Resistance and endless difficulties will arise that may endanger the reputation which the Father of Colombia has achieved by dint of so much work and effort during these thirteen years."

Riva-Agüero, the deposed president, was in Trujillo with 3,000 men. He blamed Sucre for his troubles with congress and assumed that Bolívar must also be against him. This unfortunate misunderstanding led the able patriot into a series of mistaken judgments, even to defection. Congress ordered Bolívar to arrest Riva-Agüero and prevent him from uniting with the royalists in the sierra. Bolívar arranged for his capture and had him taken to Guayaquil on his way to exile in Europe. Much damage was already done, for Riva-Agüero had aroused hatred of Colombians, and especially of Bolívar, in the Peruvian army.

The Marqués de Torre Tagle, who had succeeded Riva-Agüero as president, welcomed Bolívar as Peru's savior, and demonstrated similar enthusiasm by conferring on him the highest military authority when he entered Lima in September. Since the Peruvian army under Santa Cruz had been routed and dispersed, Bolívar realized that Sucre's Colombian troops were the only ones he could rely on. He wrote Santander that 6,000 armed and equipped troops were urgently needed. Santander, who faced many problems, somehow managed to meet Bolívar's requests. "The Liberator thinks I am God and can say 'Let it be done!' and it will be done," he grumbled. "So he asks pitilessly for arms and men, and the worst of it is that Don Simón gets all the acclaim, while the Peruvians fail to recognize the efforts of the Colombian government" — meaning himself.

Despite the chaotic state of affairs in Peru, Bolívar was delighted with Lima. Soon after his arrival he informed Santander that "I am more pleased every day with Lima. . . . The men value me and the women love me: this is most delightful; there are many pleasures about for those who can pay for them. . . . I am enchanted; of course I lack nothing."

Manuela arrived in October, and as Salvador de Madariaga wryly commented, her presence could hardly have improved Bolívar's health, for in sensuous eagerness their meeting was, in the Spanish saying, "that of hunger and appetite." But many other women covertly visited Bolívar at his Magdalena estate, and between duties and pleasures he was soon exhausted. In January, 1824, on his return to Lima after a visit to Trujillo to settle a conflict of authority with Peruvian Admiral George Guise, Bolívar fell ill with a raging fever in the village of Pativilca, where he lay for several weeks.

To Santander Bolívar attributed his illness to the long ride through the sierra, but it is more likely that it was owing both to the susceptibility to tuberculosis inherited from his mother and to his strenuous love life. "If I go for my convalescence to Lima," he admitted, "both business and pleasure will make me ill again. . . . I am very much worn out and very old. . . ."

In another letter to Santander, Bolíver spoke of losing his reason. "The Quitoans and Peruvians," he continued,

> will do nothing for their country, and therefore it is not for me to tyrannize them into salvation. . . . Hitherto I have fought for liberty; henceforward I want to fight for my glory at the cost even of the whole world. My glory consists now in no longer wielding any power or having to do with anything but myself. . . . Bonaparte, Castlereagh . . . everything falls, brought down by infamy or by misfortune — and I standing? It cannot be, and I must fall.

Callao was garrisoned by the Río de la Plata battalion of Argentines whose pay was long overdue, and who were daily on the verge of starvation. Two sergeants, who suspected that Argentine general Enrique Martínez had pocketed the troops' pay, assembled all sergeants to demand the arrears. On the night of February 4 they seized the officers, demanding 100,000 pesos and passage home.

They intercepted a message from General Martínez to the ship's captain to bring them back to be shot. After this the royalist officers imprisoned in Callao persuaded the mutineers to surrender Callao to the royalists.

On February 10 the Peruvian congress conferred dictatorial powers on Bolívar and then adjourned. Against the advice of Sucre and other friends, Bolívar accepted. Speaking of Peru, he said that it was "full of factions, and of traitors; some are for Torre Tagle, others for Riva-Agüero, others for the Spaniards, and very few for Independence. But all begin to fear me much; they also say that everything will be cured with my recipe: an ounce of lead and four drams of powder."

Bolívar was still recuperating at Pativilca when Torre Tagle delivered Lima to the royalists and sought refuge in Callao, where the royalist flag was already flying. Joaquín Mosquera, Colombia's minister to Peru, visited Bolívar at Pativilca and was so shocked at his emaciated appearance he could scarcely conceal his tears. "What will you do, my General?" he asked.

It was during the greatest crises that Bolívar's spirit was most unquenchable. "Triumph!" he replied. "In three months," he explained, "I shall have an army for the attack. I shall climb the cordillera and defeat the Spanish."

Bolívar established his headquarters at Trujillo, where he recruited and rigorously trained an army for the difficult mountain campaign. "Let us turn a deaf ear to the cries of all. . . ." he said. "War lives on despotism and is not waged with God's love. Leave nothing undone. Be terrible and adamant. Discipline the forces under your command . . . if there are no guns there are spears."

By overcoming all obstacles, Bolívar soon had an army of nearly 10,000 men ready. (A foreigner who observed this extraordinary achievement remarked, "I don't know where Bolívar got so much money, so many horses, mules, and everything else necessary to equip a large army from this depleted country. The genius of the great Bolívar is truly prodigious.") He placed Sucre in command of the allied forces, which included Colombians, a Peruvian division under General José de la Mar, and a mixed cavalry force under Argentine general Mariano Necochea and British general William Miller. Viceroy La Serna had an army of 12,000 men at Cuzco, two-thirds of the royalist army in Peru. But the royalists were also divided, for in Upper Peru General Pedro Antonio Olañeta, who was as absolutist as Ferdinand VII, had rejected La Serna's authority. When he first learned of Olañeta's rebellion, Bolívar was not surprised. "The Spanish now also suffer the influence of the evil star of Peru," he said. "The Pizarros and Almagros fought each other. La Serna fought Pezuela. Riva-Agüero fought with the Congress, Torre Tagle with Riva-Agüero, and Torre Tagle with his fatherland. Now Olañeta is fighting with La Serna, and therefore we have time to fall in line in the Palestra, armed from head to foot." He decided to take advantage of the situation. "Since receiving word of the quarrel between La Serna and Olañeta," he said, "I have decided to begin my campaign against Jauja in the month of May."

In May Bolívar entered Huailas on his way to the sierra. The usual welcome had been prepared — triumphal arches, music, church bells, and a white-gowned maiden, Manuela Madroño, who placed a garland of flowers on his head. Since he had left Manuela Sáenz de Thorne to follow at a distance, he remained in Huailas long enough to arrange for Manuela Madroño to share his hammock for the rest of the campaign in the sierra.

Shortly after this Bolívar received a detailed description of a major who planned to assassinate him. He recognized the major, and had him summoned. "I always place well officers who come to me and justify my hopes," he said.

"You will be sent as military governor to a good city." Thereafter Bolívar had nothing to fear from the would-be assassin.

The patriot army of 6,000 Colombians and 3,000 Peruvians entered the sierra by three different routes to the Jauja valley, where Canterac's royalist force was located. "I am possessed by the demon of war," Bolívar wrote, "and am about to end this fight one way or another. . . . America's genius and my fate have gone to my head." His army was thoroughly trained for mountain fighting and equipped with excellent French and British weapons — Sucre, who had supervised its training, called it the finest army that had ever fought in America, and it lived up to his expectations. Patriot morale was high, for the Peruvians were anxious to win recognition and the remaining Argentine veterans were eager to recover their former reputation. General William Miller, a veteran of the Chilean struggle for independence, commented to a friend, "I assure you that the Colombian infantry, as well as cavalry, could hold a parade in St. James Park and would attract attention."

The towering Andean cordillera was composed of three ranges that came together at the Cerro de Pasco, then forked again to enclose the highland valley of Jauja. One of the hazards for troops in the high, bleak sierra was *soroche,* or mountain sickness, which occasionally incapacitated infantrymen. Obtaining food was also a problem, but Sucre had placed stores of food at various places and had stationed trumpeters at strategic locations to guide the troops where they might lose their way. By July 15 the three divisions had reassembled at Pasco.

On August 2 Bolívar reviewed his army. "You will complete the greatest task that heaven has ever assigned to men," he told them, that of saving a whole world from slavery. Soldiers, the enemy you are about to destroy boasts of the triumphs of fourteen years. They are worthy of measuring their arms with yours, which have shone in a thousand battles. Soldiers, Peru and all of America expects peace at your hands . . . peace, the daughter of victory. Even a liberal Europe looks with pleasure on you, for the freedom of the New World is the hope of the universe.

On the afternoon of August 6 the two armies sighted each other. Canterac withdrew to protect his base at Jauja. Fearing that he might lose the opportunity to engage the royalists, Bolívar rode ahead with the cavalry and overtook Canterac on the plains of Junín. Canterac, who had the advantage of favorable terrain, ordered his infantry and artillery to continue the march to Jauja and sent his cavalry charging against the patriots' left flank and center. The Colombian cavalry, using long lances like those of the llaneros, the Granaderos a Caballo under German Colonel Philip Braun, and the Peruvian Hussars calmly met the charge. It was a confusing clash of saber and lance — no infantry took part and no shot was fired.

The battle lasted an hour and a half, when darkness descended. Four hundred royalists lay dead or wounded on the field, while the remainder fled in panic and disorder. Greatly discouraged, Canterac abandoned Jauja and marched to Cuzco, where La Serna held most of the royalist troops. To the royalist governor of Callao Canterac wrote that the flight of his cavalrymen and the numerical superiority of the patriot infantry meant that all efforts should be made to assemble a force large enough to defeat Bolívar. La Serna called in all royalist detachments except Olañeta's and prepared for the showdown.

Before meeting the combined royalist forces Bolívar awaited reinforcements from Colombia, and ordered Sucre to gather in all stragglers and convalescents. Sucre dutifully carried out the mission, then wrote Bolívar that he wished to retire, for "such a commission has been the cause of mockery and satire among those who are not my friends, and of wonder for those who esteem me." Since he was not fortunate enough to be a good soldier, he said, he wanted to be a good citizen.

Bolívar replied immediately. "I think you are entirely lacking in judgment if you believe that I wanted to insult you." He had, he said, planned to carry out the assignment himself, but he knew that Sucre, with his remarkable energy, would be better able to accomplish it. "This sensitiveness, this listening to the gossip of little men, is unworthy of you. Glory consists of being great and useful." Bolívar, who was extremely sensitive himself, must have understood Sucre's feelings. Fortunately for the patriot cause, Sucre withdrew his resignation.

The rainy season began, and little could be accomplished during the rest of August and September. In October, leaving Sucre in command of the army, to remain on the defensive or commence offensive operations at his discretion, Bolívar set out for the coast. As usual, he ordered schools opened under the control of the clergy in the towns he visited and exempted from taxation towns ruined by the royalists. The Peruvian government had negotiated a three-million-peso loan in London, and Bolívar had been warned that the money would be wasted if he did not return promptly.

Before he reached the coast Bolívar received dispatches from Bogotá — the Colombian congress had rescinded the law of 1821 giving him extraordinary powers in any theater of war. Santander implied that the congress had acted on its own initiative, but, according to O'Leary, "the truth of the matter is that this measure was adopted at the suggestion of Vice-President Santander himself, who regarded with envy Sucre's deserved advancement in the army and feared that the Liberator would confer on him the rank of general in chief should he be victorious in Peru." Bolívar was deprived of the authority to promote meritorious officers, but even more painful to him, he also lost command of Colombian troops serving in Peru.

On receiving this unwelcome news Bolívar immediately wrote to Sucre, warning him to inform the troops with great caution so their discipline would not be adversely affected. "Happy they who die before they see the end of this bloody drama," he added. "However sad our death may be, it will be gayer than this life." He soon received pleas to ignore the decision until the officers could present a petition to the congress. Bolívar refused to let them send the petition. The only outward indication of his feelings was that he suspended his personal correspondence with Santander.

Early in November Sucre learned that La Serna and the whole royalist army were approaching in an effort to encircle him and cut him off from his base at Jauja. The two armies maneuvered for the rest of the month. Finally, on December 8, they faced each other on the small plain of Ayacucho at the foot of the Condorcanqui range. The royalist army numbered over 9,000 men, while Sucre's force was less than 6,000. Early next morning, while the military bands played, royalist General Juan Antonio Monet walked to the patriot lines and talked with General José María Córdova. Some of the royalist soldiers had relatives in the patriot army, he said, and they wanted to visit them before the battle. It was agreed that the men could talk for half an hour in the open space between the lines. About fifty men from each side laid down their weapons and entered the no-man's-land between the armies to converse with brother or cousin.

A royalist brigadier general came out in search of his

younger brother, a lieutenant colonel in the Peruvian army. "Ah, my brother," he said, "how sorry I am to see you covered with ignominy."

"I didn't come here to be insulted," the younger brother replied and returned to the patriot ranks. His brother ran after him and threw his arms around him. Both wept.

After the visits were concluded both armies ate breakfast. The patriots were clad in the unspectacular uniforms and dark overcoats O'Leary had procured for them in Chile. The royalists were dressed in brightly colored uniforms. Most of the troops in both armies were natives of South America.

About half-past ten General Monet again approached the patriot lines, dressed in a splendid uniform. "General, are we ready for battle?" he asked Córdova.

"Let us fight," Córdova answered, and he left to report to Sucre. The royalists appeared completely confident because they outnumbered the patriots nearly two to one, and their position dominated the plain where the battle would be fought. But the royalist officers had convinced their men that the Colombians were inhumanly ferocious, so that many royalist soldiers were thinking more of saving their lives than of conquering.

Sucre's forces were in an exposed position, but their flanks were protected by ravines. He took the offensive, skillfully maneuvering his forces so as to exert the heaviest pressure wherever it was needed. The royalist division that first gave way was the one that had fraternized with the patriots earlier. Because the royalists — with an army superior in numbers, training, and artillery — were thoroughly routed, some have suspected them of selling out to the patriots before the battle began. Sucre's report gives only a sketchy outline of events while Canterac's is devoted primarily to justifying his defeat and surrender. Sucre's terms were unusually generous, so the suspicions of prearrangements may be justified. The royalists needed a face-saving solution to an impossible situation. The viceroy, fifteen generals, sixteen colonels, and more than 550 other officers surrendered.

If the royalists did, indeed, make only a token gesture of fighting in order to surrender with honor, it would not be surprising. In the previous year a French army had marched into Spain and restored Ferdinand VII to absolute rule; liberals were again harassed and persecuted, and many Spanish officers were of liberal persuasion. To them the idea of fighting Spanish Americans to preserve Ferdinand's domination was distasteful, and it had caused the rift between Olañeta and La Serna. After the defeat at Ayacucho, only Olañeta's army remained at large in Upper Peru. Immediately after Ayacucho Sucre wrote Bolívar: "The war is ended. The freedom of Peru is complete. As a reward for me I ask that you reserve your friendship for me." He sent Colonel Celedonio Medina to report the victory, but Indians who had been encouraged to kill patriot soldiers stoned him to death as he crossed a bridge.

Not long after his defeat at Ayacucho, General Canterac wrote Bolívar, "As one who knows glorious deeds even in the face of personal defeat, I feel I must congratulate Your Excellency for having finished your assignment in Peru by the battle of Ayacucho."

Bolívar issued a proclamation giving Sucre full credit for the stunning victory and naming him field marshal in the Peruvian army as well as "Liberator of Peru." "Sucre has won the most brilliant victory of the American War," he wrote Santander. "I deem him fully worthy of it." The Peruvian congress would soon meet, he added, and the royalist garrison in Callao would soon fall. Then he would be free to depart for Europe, he said, for he was tired of ruling. "Everybody is burning me with reproaches about my ambition and my wanting to be crowned; the French say it; in Chile and Buenos Aires, they say it; here they say it, not to speak of the anonymous paper of Caracas. I want no more glories. I have only one-third of my life left, and I want to live." Actually, he had only about one-ninth of his life left. He asked for 100,000 pesos, for he was living on borrowed money — he had refused the salary that Peru offered, and that from Colombia did not arrive. The reason he had not received it, he said, was owing to Dr. Azuero, "an old enemy of mine but a friend of yours." (Azuero was the one whose flowery speech Bolívar had cut short when he entered Bogotá in 1819.)

Announcing the convocation of the national assembly for February 10, 1825, Bolívar declared, "It is time for me to fulfill the promise I have given you, namely, the abolition of dictatorship on the very day that victory decided your destiny. . . . The day on which your Parliament convenes will be the day of my glory, the day on which my most ardent desires have been fulfilled, the day on which, once and for all, I resign my rule." A few months earlier he had resigned the presidency of Gran Colombia, but the congress had refused to accept his resignation.

When the Peruvian National Assembly met on February 10, it, too, rejected Bolívar's resignation amid a farrago of patriotic, impassioned speeches. Bolívar declared that he could not accept an office that conflicted with his conscience, although he was willing to continue serving "with sword and heart." His goal was the creation of a great federation in which Gran Colombia, Peru, and other nations would join forces. He warned the congress of the danger of entrusting supreme power to one man, especially a foreigner. He spoke of returning to Colombia — the congress was stunned and crowds in the streets implored him not to desert Peru in a time of need. "Here they link me with Mercury's staff which had the power to link in friendship all the serpents which might have devoured each other," he wrote. "Nobody gets along with anybody, but everyone gets along with me."

A large delegation from congress waited on Bolívar, insisting that he accept a decree bestowing unlimited authority on him until it reconvened in 1826. He was empowered to delegate authority in the interim. He agreed to serve as dictator for another year, but when the congress voted a gift of one million pesos he asked that it be given to the city of Caracas for reconstruction. He also allocated some of the money to pay British educator Joseph Lancaster to promote the education of the children of Caracas, but since Peruvian agents in London failed to cover the drafts Bolívar eventually had to pay 20,000 pesos out of his personal funds. He was equally concerned over improving education in Peru, and when Simón Rodríguez arrived in Lima, Bolívar made his old tutor responsible for introducing the Lancastrian system in southern Peru.

Bolívar governed Peru through three ministers, the Peruvians Hipólito Unánue and José Sánchez Carrión, and Colombian general Tomás de Heres. Peruvians hated Heres, Bolívar's minister of war, as well as Bolívar's military secretary, José Gabriel Pérez. This dislike gave rise to a typically Spanish play on words: *Heres más malo que Pérez* sounded when spoken the same as *Eres más malo que Pérez,* meaning "You are worse than Pérez."

The year 1825 was for Bolívar a year of fulfillment, perhaps the most delightful of his life, for he was at the pinnacle of fame and power. He lived like a monarch in the splendid country estate of La Magdalena. The men of Lima were eager to serve him — the women were even more eager to win recognition as his lovers. Despite Manuela Sáenz de Thorne's affectionate and jealous attentions, and although she remained unrivaled as the Liberator's favorite, Bolívar received and regaled so many Limeño women that gossips referred to La Magdalena as "The Liberator's Seraglio." On one occasion Manuela discovered a diamond bracelet in Bolívar's bed and scratched his neck and face so fiercely he had to remain in seclusion for a week. The official report was that the Liberator was suffering from a severe cold.

During this period Manuela's husband constantly tried to persuade her to return to him. She rejected his offers of money as well as his efforts to win her back. On one occasion her patience wore thin, and she replied in a forceful letter.

No, no, no! — ask me no more, man, for the love of God! Why do you make me write to you in defiance of my resolve not to do it! Come now — what do you gain thereby except making me tell you a thousand times No!

Sir, you are excellent, you are inimitable, never shall I deny that of you, but listen, my friend! — to leave *you* in order to go to General Bolívar is something, to leave a husband without your qualities would be nothing!

Do you really think that I, the mistress of Bolívar for seven years and assured of possessing his heart, would prefer to be the wife of the Father, the Son or the Holy Trinity? If there is one thing I regret it is that you are not even a better man than you are, in order that I might have had the added satisfaction of leaving you. I know perfectly well that there is no power that can unite me to Bolívar under the auspices of what you call honor. But — do you think me less honored because he is my lover and not my husband? Ah, I do not worry about social conventions, invented by men for the purpose of tormenting each other!

Leave me alone, my dear Englishman. Let us make another arrangement: in heaven we'll get married again, but on this earth — never! Do you think this is a bad idea?

If so, you are a very hard man to satisfy. Up in the celestial regions we shall live an angelic life, an entirely spiritual life — (for, as a man, you are a bit dull). Up in heaven everything will be English style for monotony in life is reserved for your nation — (in love, I mean, for who is as clever as the English in commercial and maritime things?). You English like love without pleasures, conversation without grace. You must walk at a slow pace, salute reverentially, sit down and get up carefully, joke without laughing. Such things are formalities for the gods — as for me, unhappy mortal that I am, always laughing at myself, at you, at all this English solemnity, what a bad time I should have in heaven! Quite as bad as if I went to live in England or Constantinople, because the English seem to me tyrannical with women — though you were not a tyrant toward me. You were, however, more jealous than a Portuguese! I don't want that sort of thing! Have I not good taste?

Well, no more joking. Formally, without laughing, with all the seriousness, truthfulness and purity of an Englishwoman, I tell you *that I shall not go back to you again!* The fact that you are an Anglican and I am an atheist is the principal religious obstacle, the fact that I am in love with another man is the biggest and most important obstacle of all. Come now, acknowledge that I have thought this out seriously!

> Invariably your friend,
> Manuela

Bolívar's fame was by no means limited to South America. The descendants of George Washington, calling him "the second Washington of the New World," sent him as a token of their appreciation a gold medal that had been struck after the victory at Yorktown and had been a prized possession of their illustrious forebear. They also suggested to Lafayette that he write Bolívar. British Foreign Secretary George Canning wrote him in December of 1824 to convey his government's recognition of Gran Colombia. Quixotic Lord Byron was preparing to sail to "the country of Bolívar" to offer his services when he learned that the wars had ended; still seeking romantic adventure, he joined the Greeks in their struggle for independence from Turkey. The United Provinces of Río de la Plata sent a delegation to congratulate Bolívar and to seek his help in a war with Brazil. All of these gestures of appreciation and recognition from near and far were most gratifying to Bolívar. Many of his friends spoke constantly of creating a monarchy for him, and the word "crown" frequently appeared in his letters. Bolívar could not have avoided considering the matter, but the "glory" that had ever been his goal was that of the conquering hero, not of an overweight king. There is no doubt that he favored authoritarian government, for anarchy threatened in all parts of Spanish America. After Ayacucho he had to discover new adventures to maintain and enhance his "glory," but warfare, not a crown, was what constantly appealed to him.

For Bolívar the year 1825 was also one of feverish administrative activity — promoting education and the economy, and dispensing justice by a series of decrees. He created an economic society to promote prosperity and established a commission of prominent jurists to write new civil and criminal codes. In the capital of each department he ordered the establishment of a normal school based on the Lancastrian system, for the purpose of extending education to all social classes. He decreed that children of the poor were to receive free instruction. He attempted to relieve the Indians of oppression and ordered community lands divided among their families — lands that could not be alienated before 1850.

A Dane in the French service, Admiral van Dockun, described Bolívar at this time. His mien and attitude were those of a perfect soldier. His large black moustache, beginning to gray like his abundant hair, gave him a martial air that contrasted sharply with his feeble voice and wasted frame. His face was wan, dark, and sunburned, showing traces of the hardships he had undergone. His lofty forehead and the earnestness of his manner called for veneration, "so that despite oneself one felt bound to bow before him, though he was free of any presumption or despotism. He impressed me as a great man." Admiral van Dockun, who was present during an exchange between Bolívar and an overbearing French diplomat, declared, "I never saw intellectual superiority so plainly manifest as in that famous interview."

In Peru Bolívar's activities continued at the same hectic pace. After the Colombian and Peruvian congresses had rejected his resignations, he was still tortured by the imputations of his enemies that his devotion to liberty and independence was merely the by-product of personal ambition. In the spring of 1825, nevertheless, he set out on a tour of the southern departments of Peru, for the purpose of improving conditions, removing abuses, and promoting education. His tour was reminiscent of the visitation of sixteenth-century Viceroy Francisco de Toledo, who spent two years moving from town to town, righting wrongs, issuing edicts, and in general driving local officials to distraction.

At Arequipa solicitous city officials presented Bolívar with an excellent horse luxuriously adorned with gold trappings, but this did not prevent him, as they may have hoped, from scrutinizing carefully the organization and administration of the department. In June he continued to Cuzco, where triumphal arches and another horse with gold trappings awaited him.

In Cuzco Bolívar issued decrees similar to those he had issued in Lima benefiting Indians. He founded an academy for girls, endowing it with sufficient revenue to operate. He also established an orphanage and a home for old and poor people. With the approval of ecclesiastical officials he reduced the number of convents and assigned their buildings and revenues to charitable works. He observed that the Cuzco region was productive but completely isolated for lack of good roads. He ordered two new roads opened and personally marked out the routes, but the projects were never completed. He also ordered an aqueduct to be built for the city.

While Bolívar was making his viceregal tour, the war in Upper Peru was finally brought to a successful conclusion. After the surrender of most of the royalist army at Ayacucho, the only enemy forces remaining were Olañeta's army in Upper Peru and the royalist garrison at Callao, which was under siege.

Casimiro Olañeta, the general's unscrupulous, opportunistic nephew and secretary, surmised that the patriot army would soon triumph over his die-hard uncle and prepared for his own survival by opening communications with Bolívar and Sucre. He persuaded the patriot guerrilla leader, General Miguel Lanza, that General Olañeta had gone over to the patriot side. Lanza soon learned that Casimiro was a *dos caras,* or two-faced, not to be trusted under any circumstances.

Sucre was reluctant to become embroiled in the perplexing situation in Upper Peru and asked to be relieved of his command. By January, 1825, however, it was clear that General Olañeta would not accept the Ayacucho capitulation terms. He accused La Serna of treason and vowed to triumph in the sacred cause of king and religion if he had to fight to the last man. To gain time for obtaining needed arms and reinforcements, however, he concluded a four-month truce with Sucre's representative, Colonel Antonio Elizalde. He immediately sent his nephew Casimiro and General Pablo Echeverría to purchase arms being sent to the port of Iquique by royalists in the archipelago of Chiloé off the coast of southern Chile. Echeverría had accepted the surrender terms in which all royalist officers had sworn never to take up arms against the patriots. By joining Olañeta, Echeverría had broken his oath.

Shortly before departing on this mission Casimiro wrote a confidential letter to Sucre, informing him that he had manipulated his uncle into rebelling against La Serna to weaken the royalist army. His uncle had signed the truce, he said, merely to gain time. His army numbered 4,000 poorly armed men whose morale had deteriorated. He assured Sucre that if the patriots crossed the Río Desaguadero the royalist army would collapse. Colonels Pedro Arraya and Carlos Medinaceli, furthermore, were ready to come over to the patriots at the appropriate time.

Casimiro and Echeverría left for Tarapacá with 10,000 pesos to secure the arms at the port of Iquique. In Tarapacá Casimiro seized Echeverría, took his documents and money, and turned him over to local officials with instructions to deliver him to patriot authorities in Arequipa. Then he hurried to Puno to meet Sucre, giving him Echeverría's papers and warning him to intercept the arms shipment from Iquique.

Sucre was favorably impressed by Casimiro's facility with words and for this reason ignored General Lanza's warning that the turncoat was not to be trusted and should be deported to a distant country. Both Sucre and Lanza would regret the former's failure to heed this sound advice. Casimiro remained close to Sucre, advising him on how to deal with his uncle, and arranging, through his own agents, a mutiny of royalist troops.

Furious at Echeverría's violation of his oath, Sucre ordered officials in Arequipa to have him shot immediately. When Echeverría's wife pleaded for her husband's life,

Sucre relented and sent a courier with orders to suspend the execution, but the message, to Sucre's deep sorrow, arrived too late.

On entering La Paz on February 9, 1825, Sucre issued a decree which laid the groundwork for the independence of Upper Peru. During most of the colonial era the region had been part of the Viceroyalty of Peru, but with the creation of the Viceroyalty of Río de la Plata in 1776–77, it was transferred to that administration. The Argentines, eager to retain the rich silver region, had sent a number of expeditions to drive the royalists out, but all had failed. Despite these failures Argentines still regarded Upper Peru as part of the United Provinces of Río de la Plata.

Sucre had come, his proclamation stated, to free them from Spanish rule, not to intervene in their domestic affairs. It was necessary, however, to establish some governmental authority, and he would provide it until an assembly met in Oruro in April to decide on a course of action. The decree of February 9 made provisions for electing the national assembly that would declare Upper Peru independent.

Hoping to avoid further bloodshed, Sucre waited for stiff-necked General Olañeta to admit that his was a lost cause. Through Casimiro's manipulations, a number of royalist units deserted, and on April 1 Colonel Medinaceli led his troops in an attack in which General Olañeta was fatally wounded under mysterious circumstances. Sucre suspected foul play, and it seems likely the stubborn old absolutist was shot down by his own troops. With his death royalist resistance in the sierra ended.

The national assembly did not meet until July, and then in Chuquisaca rather than Oruro. Bolívar had been disturbed by Sucre's proclamation, which he viewed as an invitation to separatism. The Spanish Americans had agreed after 1810 that the colonial administrative divisions

— viceroyalties, captaincies general, and presidencies —
would, under the principle of *uti possidetis,* form the terri-
torial framework of the new nations. As Bolívar wrote
Sucre on learning of his decree of February 9, "what has
come to be recognized as a principle of international law
in America, namely, that the republican governments are
founded within the boundaries of former viceroyalties,
captaincies general, and presidencies," made it necessary
to study thoroughly the sensitive question of Argentina's
claim to jurisdiction in Upper Peru.

When the assembly met, Casimiro Olañeta and several
of his *dos caras* associates dominated the debates. Some
wanted to attach the country to Peru, but Casimiro and
his friends prevailed, and on August 6 the assembly rejected joining either Peru or Argentina in favor of independence. A bombastic declaration of independence,
which had been prepared in advance, was read. Then the
delegates voted to name the new nation after Bolívar, to
flatter him and thereby undermine his opposition to the
region's separation from Argentina. The assembly also
invited Bolívar to draw up a basic code of laws.

In September Bolívar visited Upper Peru, where he
received a horse, gold keys, and a crown of gold and diamonds. "This reward belongs to the victor," he said, "and
that is why I am turning it over to the hero of Ayacucho."
In one of the happiest days of his life, Bolívar fulfilled an
earlier vow by climbing the famed silver mountain of
Potosí and unfurling the flags of Gran Colombia, Peru,
and Río de la Plata. It was a fitting climax to his military
career.

SIX

Descent from Potosí

WHILE IN UPPER PERU, Bolívar introduced judicial reforms, abolished Indian tribute and granted Indians full citizenship, and ordered that academies and primary schools be opened in each province. He appointed Simón Rodríguez director of public education and charitable institutions, unsuitable though the old man's theories and methods were for the isolated Indian and mestizo population of the bleak altiplano. Bolívar also issued regulations to improve agriculture and for the distribution of land in Santa Cruz province. To revive mining he abolished special mining taxes and decreed the establishment of mining schools in Potosí and La Paz. He reduced import duties to discourage smuggling, urged the improvement of roads to stimulate commerce, and established an economic society to promote various enterprises. It should not be assumed that much positive action resulted from his edicts, although he urged Sucre to carry out the proposed improvements.

On August 11, 1825, the new nation was named *República Bolívar* (later changed to Bolivia) and Bolívar was

designated as its protector, with supreme powers whenever he was in the country. Sucre was also honored by
having the old capital, Chuquisaca, renamed Sucre.

Before leaving Chuquisaca early in January, 1826, Bolívar addressed the assembly to explain the various provisions of the constitution he planned, and set May 25 as the
date for convening the congress. Then, delegating supreme authority to Sucre, he departed. As on other occasions when Bolívar had introduced sweeping changes, the
dust quickly settled and the customary ways were restored
once he was out of sight.

While Bolívar was in Bolivia conspiracies became widespread in Peru, and the congressional elections clearly
expressed discontent with him, for although the majority
of deputies elected favored his government, his opponents
and even known royalists won seats in some regions. Before he reached Lima early in February the royalists in
Callao surrendered and were given liberal terms on orders
from Bolívar. On his arrival at his Magdalena estate, political agitation seemed to subside.

Despite the many problems that faced him, Bolívar
found time to write the constitution that the Chuquisaca
assembly had requested. He aimed to create a system that
could provide stability and unity while preventing revolution and chaos. The government he envisaged would be
popular and representative in form and theory, with four
main branches — electoral, legislative, executive, and judicial.

The electoral branch was Bolívar's own invention.
Every ten citizens would choose one elector, so this branch
would embrace one-tenth of literate citizens. The electors
would select members of the legislature and nominate
candidates for provincial offices.

The legislature was to be composed of three houses —
the Chambers of Tribunes, Senators, and Censors. The

censors, who would hold office for life, were to settle disputes between the other two chambers, exercise moral power, prevent violations of the constitution, protect freedom of the press, and in general play the deity. The censors' duties, considering the time and conditions, were awesome indeed, beyond the capacity of the mere mortals who were selected.

The president was also to hold office for life, and to choose his successor. Most of the administration would be left to the vice-president and various cabinet secretaries. The judiciary was to be absolutely independent. The Bolivarian constitution declared an end to slavery and abolished entail, so that the great estates could be broken up. Bolívar sent the constitution to Chuquisaca and asked Sucre to urge its adoption.

The project that captivated Bolívar most at this time was his plan for a federation of Latin-American states, with himself at its head. Earlier he had sent agents to various countries inviting them to send delegates to a meeting in Panama in 1826, a meeting later referred to as the First Pan-American Congress. He was convinced that he must create a strong foundation for hemispheric security and solidarity, which would be his crowning achievement.

As early as 1815 Bolívar had spoken of a great confederation of Spanish-American states whose representatives would meet regularly in Panama, but at that time it was only a vague concept. The idea grew slowly, stimulated by the union of Venezuela and New Granada into a Gran Colombia that would soon embrace Ecuador as well. In 1821 he had sent Joaquín Mosquera to the south and Miguel Santamaría to Mexico to invite the new governments to join in the campaigns against the remaining royalist forces and also to send delegates to a federal congress in Panama when the time was appropriate.

On Bolívar's return to Lima in December, 1824, he had circulated a letter among the various governments, including that of the Brazilian empire, again inviting them to send representatives to Panama and emphasizing the importance of the meeting for their future well-being. He instructed the Colombian minister in Washington to discuss the Panama Congress with United States officials, and if their reaction was favorable, to invite the United States to send a delegation. British Foreign Minister George Canning feared that the congress would outlaw monarchy in the Western Hemisphere, but the Colombian minister to London assured him that the emperor of Brazil had been invited to send delegates, and he extended the same invitation to the British government.

The various delegates arrived in Panama at intervals during the year preceding June, 1826, when the Panama Congress convened. Britain and Holland sent men to act as advisers without participating in debates. Only the representatives of Gran Colombia, Guatemala, Mexico, and Peru were present, for Argentina had refused to send a deputy, Chile was unable to because of near-anarchy, and Brazil simply failed to respond. The delegate from the United States died en route, and his replacement arrived after the sessions had adjourned in mid-July. The meetings were generally harmonious, and the delegates signed a treaty creating a permanent confederation, agreeing to meet in Tacubaya, Mexico, annually in time of war and every other year in peacetime. Other states were to be admitted if they endorsed the treaty within a year after its ratification by the governments of those present.

The results of the Panama Congress were disappointing to Bolívar, who had refused to interfere in any way despite the urgings of Santander and influential men in other states. Though tempted to attend and to present his views in person, Bolívar had abstained because he feared that his presence would be misinterpreted. But owing to his unrivaled influence, it seems certain that if he had taken part in the congress it would have been much more productive with regard to his long-range goals, although its work, like many of his other efforts, might have been ephemeral, to crumble during his own lifetime. He was far from satisfied with the treaties that had been signed, and he suspected that transferring future meetings from Panama to Tacubaya would enable Mexico and the United States to dominate them. The Congress of Panama accomplished so little that Bolívar accepted the fact that his dream of a great confederation of states in the Western Hemisphere was chimerical under present circumstances.

Bolívar's ideas concerning international arbitration of disputes in the Americas and common defense of the hemisphere were sound but inappropriate for that age. Refusing to admit his disappointment, he declared that the failure of the Panama Congress was no surprise. "I called the Congress of Panama," he declared, "in order to create a sensation. It was my ambition to bring the name of Colombia and the other South American republics to the attention of the whole world. . . . I never believed that an American League, comparable to the Holy Alliance . . . would result from its deliberations."

His plans for a South American league shattered, despite his lame denial, Bolívar now aimed at creating a Federation of the Andes. His influence over the regions from Venezuela to Bolivia was unrivaled, and his popularity extended to Chile and Argentina. This situation led some of his friends in the various regions to talk of creating an empire with Bolívar at the head.

Among those favoring creation of an empire was José M. Pando, who had been recalled from the Panama Congress to head the Ministry of Finance. Pando was alarmed over reports that Spain had assembled a large force in Cuba to reconquer her former colonies, and he was convinced that Britain would not interfere if the Holy Alliance aided Spain. Only by establishing an empire from the Orinoco to Potosí, he asserted, could the former colonies hope to defend themselves against the forces of Europe.

Bolívar preferred a tightly knit alliance of republics, each retaining its own government and sending deputies to a federal congress which would manage foreign affairs and defense. He envisioned himself as Protector of the Federation, which would have only one flag and one army. Theoretically this could be an effective and workable arrangement among cooperative states, but in the new nations the spirit of rivalry overshadowed the spirit of cooperation. One problem was that Bolívar could not be everywhere at once, and each country demanded his presence. And, as O'Leary remarked, when one man is so preeminent, ambitious men can hope to rival him only by bringing him down to their level by destroying his reputation and influence. This, he said, was Bolívar's fate.

Late in 1825 Páez and other Venezuelans, seeing anarchy spreading around them, concluded that the republican form was a failure, that a monarchy was needed. Páez wrote Bolívar: "This country is similar to France on the day when the great Napoleon was in Egypt and was called upon by the most famous men of the Revolution to save France. You should become the Bonaparte of South America because 'this country is not the country of Washington.' "

María Antonia, Bolívar's sister, was aware of these schemes, and as usual freely offered her advice in unequivocal terms. "They send you now a commission to offer you the crown," she wrote. "Receive them as they deserve to be received, because the proposal is infamous. . . . Tell them always what you told them in Cumaná in 1814, that you will be the Liberator or nothing. This title is your real one; it is the title that will now preserve your reputation built at the cost of untold sacrifice. You should repudiate anyone who offers you a crown, because such a one is interested only in your downfall."

Much as he admired Napoleon, Bolívar did not envy his fate. "Colombia is not France," he wrote Páez,

> and I am not Napoleon . . . nor do I wish to be. Neither shall I emulate Caesar, even less Iturbide. Such examples seem unworthy of my glory. The title of Liberator is beyond any reward ever offered to human pride. . . . A throne would produce terror as much by its height as by its splendor. Equality would be obliterated, and the colored race, in the face of a new aristocracy, would feel that their rights had been entirely lost. . . . I confess frankly that this plan is inappropriate for you, for me, and for the country.

Reforms, he added, should not be considered before 1831, since the Constitution of Cúcuta had been accepted for ten years.

The talk of crowning Bolívar continued, despite his outspoken opposition. "My enemies and my foolish friends have talked so much about this crown," he complained, "that I will be expelled from Colombia and America. They refuse to believe that I detest power as greatly as I love glory. Glory does not imply command, but the practice of great virtue. I wanted freedom and fame; I have achieved both. What else can I wish?" He sent the letter rejecting the crown to Santander, that he might read it and forward it to Páez.

Having no heirs with whom to create a dynasty, Bolívar had no reason for wanting a crown. He preferred the presidency for life, surrounded by a moral and intellectual elite rather than a traditional aristocracy. But his greatness was as an indomitable military commander, and once the wars were concluded he was no longer in his element. He clung to his dream of a Federation of the Andes despite all objections — since there were no more battles to be fought, this would be his last glorious achievement. Santander regarded union between Colombia and Peru ridiculous, and others opposed it because they could see no advantages to themselves. Bolívar's dream of creating a powerful and prosperous union, the southern counterpart of the United States, ignored geographical, racial, and human obstacles as well as the indifference of those he would raise to greatness. Like the vision that inspired the Panama Congress, his dream of a Federation of the Andes was doomed to oblivion.

Everywhere opinion of the Bolivarian constitution was sharply divided, but its author had no misgivings as to its merits and suitability for all Spanish-American republics. Writing Sucre to urge him to push for its adoption by Bolivians, he called it a constitution "that has achieved a perfection almost beyond any hope. Pando says it is divine, the work of genius, and as perfect as possible. Pando is a man incapable of flattery." He went on to describe his work as "the ark of alliance, the compromise between Europe and America, between the army and the people, democracy and autocracy, empire and republic. . . ."

Because of Bolívar's enormous prestige and virtually absolute power, he heard nothing but praise for his constitution. No one who visited him at Magdalena said anything that was less than laudatory about it. Despite this, his friend and aide O'Leary stated, "In no case was he more eager for the opinion of the public and of individuals than he was in the matter of his proposed constitution." When José Joaquín de Olmedo sailed for England, Bolívar asked him to read the constitution and tell him frankly what he found wrong with it.

No one anywhere gave Bolívar a frank opinion or

criticism of his constitution. "Even General Santander," said O'Leary, "who later distinguished himself by the virulence of his opposition to both the author and the constitution itself, said in a letter to Bolívar that he considered it to be 'liberal and popular, strong and vigorous.' " He stated this, O'Leary added,

> in order to have the basis for comparison with later events and to show fully the vicious conduct of Bolívar's opponents and the almost complete lack of honest principles of logic in the hostile criticism later aimed at his reputation. The very same men who had been most lavish with their praise in the days of Bolívar's splendor were the first ones to berate and slander him when fortune no longer favored him. If the Bolivian Constitution deserved the severe criticism to which it has been subjected recently, why was there not a single Patriot in Peru who would point out its defects?

Bolívar remained far too long in Lima, considering the situation in Bogotá and Caracas, but he reveled in the life at Magdalena, in his unrivaled power, and in the insistence of prominent Peruvians that he remain. Thoughtful men had no doubts that anarchy would follow in the wake of Bolívar's departure. Even while he was there, opposition to him and to the Colombian troops called in to liberate Peru produced outbreaks and mutinies. Memories were short, and Bolívar and the Colombian troops were soon viewed as oppressors.

Because of the increasing troubles in Gran Colombia, Bolívar knew that he could not delay much longer. He received pleas from Pedro Briceño Méndez, Urdaneta, and many others to return and restore order. In July, 1826, General Andrés Santa Cruz, a member of the Council of State, had to leave Lima to suppress a mutiny of hussars in Huancayo, who proclaimed as their purpose the freeing of Peru from oppression by Colombians. The rebels committed many outrages before they were subdued. Bolívar knew that the same pretext would be seized by other Peruvian army units. He announced that he would depart as soon as Santa Cruz returned.

Peruvians who feared the anarchy that would break out the moment Bolívar left the country besieged him with petitions to stay. The electoral college hastily adopted the Bolivarian constitution and declared him president for life. When "a considerable number of beautiful and respectable Peruvian ladies . . . surrounded him and demanded with the most insistent entreaties that he remain in Peru," he smiled broadly and appeared to give in. But the news from Bogotá and Caracas convinced him that he had already dallied too long in Lima. "As long as the liberators congregate around me," he said prophetically, "Colombia will remain united; afterward there will be civil war."

Relations between Páez and Santander — between Venezuela and Colombia — had seriously and steadily deteriorated. One of the incidents that contributed to an outright break between the two countries was the case of Venezuelan Colonel Leonardo Infante, a Negro officer who was the hero of many battles but was disliked and feared because of his violent nature. Late in 1824 an officer named Francisco Perdomo was murdered in Bogotá. There were no witnesses, but it was believed that Perdomo and Infante had quarreled over a woman. A military court tried Infante and condemned him to death on suspicion alone. When the case was reviewed the court was divided in opinion, but the death sentence was upheld on the basis of a law requiring only a simple majority. The president of the high court of justice, Dr. Miguel Peña, himself a mulatto, properly refused to sign a sentence he considered notoriously illegal, although Bolívar wrote advising him not to take an extreme position. Peña was suspended for refusing to sign the sentence.

Protesting his innocence, Infante was executed. After the execution Santander appeared on horseback to harangue the troops in the presence of the corpse. O'Leary, who hated Santander, called this action an unbecoming display of vanity on the part of the head of the government, especially as Santander was known to be a personal enemy of the victim. Since he could have commuted the sentence, Santander's conduct was viewed as an ignoble act of vengeance.

Peña made a brilliant defense of his actions, but while he was under suspension, as an added insult he was forced to recompense the judge who replaced him. He left immediately for Valencia, burning for an opportunity to avenge himself.

The final break between Páez and the Santander government grew out of an attempt to recruit militia troops needed to suppress the roving bands pillaging the country around Caracas. In 1824 the Venezuelan government had issued a decree requiring service in the militia for all men of sixteen to fifty years of age except those usually exempt because of their professions. The people of Caracas regarded the decree with contempt. When Páez informed the government of the alarming state of public opinion, he was told not to take any action that would lead to civil disturbances, so he simply refrained from enforcing the decree.

Late in 1825 the military commander of the province of Caracas warned Páez that the city was defenseless and that there was immediate danger of a Negro uprising. To meet the emergency Páez had no choice but to call up the militia. He ordered all men of draft age to report, but the people of Caracas ignored the summons. The call-up was repeated in January, 1826, but only a few men complied.

Páez, who was accustomed to unquestioned obedience, angrily ordered the regular units to round up all men found on the streets and take them to the barracks. The troops did not enter private homes, but there was a bitter reaction throughout the city.

The intendant of Caracas, General Juan Escalona, asked Páez to remove his troops from the city, assuring him that all eligible men would report voluntarily. Páez agreed, but Escalona made an exaggerated report to the government in Bogotá, falsely accusing Páez of brutality against citizens. Because Páez had enemies among the Venezuelans in the Gran Colombian congress, they seized the opportunity to bring reckless charges against him simply to insult him. Even worse, the senate suspended Páez and ordered Escalona to replace him as military commander. "We must confess that Morillo spoke the truth to you in Santa Ana," Páez wrote Bolívar, "when he said he had rendered a signal service to the Republic by killing off all the lawyers, but we must accuse ourselves of the sin of having left uncompleted Morillo's work, for we have not done as much with those we still had at hand."

In April, 1826, Páez received official notice of his suspension and orders from Santander to surrender his command to Escalona, who had brought the charges against him. His anger was uncontrollable, and Dr. Peña now saw in Páez his instrument for vengeance. On reading the letter suspending Páez, he exclaimed, "No matter which way you look at this paper, it means only one thing — revolution."

Páez wrote the government in Bogotá that he would turn over his command to Escalona, but agitators frightened off officials who tried to enforce law and order, and declared Páez restored to his command. Encouraged, Páez took an oath "to observe and enforce the established laws, but not to obey the new orders from the Bogotá government." He sent a message to Bolívar urging him to come quickly to avoid civil war. He complained bitterly against Santander and again urged Bolívar to accept a crown.

Santander, who had assured Bolívar that the country was peaceful and without factions, was urged to call a special session of the congress to request Bolívar to return and take charge of the government. Santander toyed with the idea of ordering an invasion of Venezuela, but Minister of War Soublette convinced him that it would be a fatal error. Through the newspapers Santander made such vitriolic attacks on Páez and other Venezuelans that reconciliation was impossible. He finally informed Bolívar of the true state of affairs.

It was late in June when Bolívar learned of the action Páez had taken in Valencia, but the reports were more confusing than enlightening. Bolívar's only conclusion was that the solution to the problem of unity and stability was the adoption of the Bolivarian constitution. He recommended that Colombia consider it and adopt it, as Peru and Guayaquil had done. Fearing a fate such as that of Piar, Páez and Peña courted a following among the *pardo* castes — María Antonia called them "pardocrats" — and a racial conflict threatened.

Bolívar sent O'Leary to reconcile Santander and Páez, but only the former appeared willing to compromise. O'Leary informed Páez that Bolívar would be deeply distressed if he did anything to disrupt the peace. Fearing that he had already gone too far to turn back safely, Páez rebuffed O'Leary, who reported to Bolívar that the llanero chieftain was "an immoral, malicious, insidious man. . . ." At the risk of losing Bolívar's friendship, O'Leary openly expressed fear that he might condone the rupture Páez had made with Gran Colombia. He was equally solicitous of Bolívar's reputation when warning him against accepting a crown, for many of those who recommended it sought his ruin. Bolívar's reaction was a temporary coolness toward O'Leary.

When Páez and other officers swore to accept no more orders from Bogotá, the break between Venezuela and Colombia was complete. In a long letter to Bolívar, Páez blamed all of Venezuela's troubles on Santander and begged Bolívar to settle the dispute between them, meaning that he should reprimand Santander. Everyone relied on Bolívar to work miracles at such times, although some hoped to see him fail.

It was with more regret than pleasure that Bolívar prepared for the return to Gran Colombia. "Colombia calls on me and I obey," he said at last, having already procrastinated too long. In August, 1825, Santander had written, "As long as I live I shall continue to advise you never, under any circumstances, to govern during a period of peace. No, my dear General, no one can be a real friend of yours if he advises you to govern ignorant people." Whatever Santander's purpose or motive, this was sound advice, for Bolívar was temperamentally unsuited to administration, especially when he would have to contend with a corrupt congress that was infecting the nation. "I am not capable of playing on such a complicated keyboard," Bolívar declared. "I would break it." Having been accustomed to the exercise of dictatorial powers since 1814, opposition drove Bolívar into a rage.

By September, 1826, when Bolívar finally left Peru and sailed to Guayaquil on his way to Bogotá, it was far too late to close the breach between Páez and Santander. He turned over charge of Peruvian affairs to men he trusted and left most of the Colombian army there. Some Peruvians, fearing chaos, mourned his departure, but others were conspiring to assassinate him if he remained. "Your presence is absolutely necessary," Santander had written him, believing that he would bring the Colombian Third Division and reduce Venezuela to subservience. It was no easy decision for Bolívar to give up the pleasures of Lima and his awesome power there to plunge into an inferno of hatreds and jealousies. "I swear with the utmost sincerity," he wrote Santander, "that I fear my beloved fatherland more than the rest of America. I believe myself more capable of ruling the New World than of ruling Venezuela."

In Bogotá, the congress, which was itself deservedly suspect, became suspicious of the soldiers. It failed in its efforts to disenfranchise them but did reduce their pay by one-third. While a civil-military clash was in the making, the congress also attacked the privileges of the clergy.

In 1824 Colombia had negotiated a thirty-million-peso loan under extremely unfavorable terms. During the next year the funds had disappeared — public opinion held Santander responsible. What Bolívar faced on his return, then, was a discontented population, a demoralized army, a worried and dissatisfied clergy, a corrupt legislature, an empty treasury, and an executive generally believed to have had a key part in the dissipation of funds. Groups of frustrated people were ready to rebel, to strike out blindly, for with the royalists gone it was difficult to identify the enemy. In this situation republican institutions, which were still new and strange to the people, meant nothing.

Charges were twice leveled against Francisco Montoya and Manuel Arrubla, who as Colombian agents had negotiated the loan, but owing to Santander's zealous defense of them the charges were dropped on both occasions. Then Santander proposed to congress to contract for another loan. "The speculators had," Mosquera wrote Bolívar in April, 1826, "bought up huge quantities of national bonds at a fifth or sixth of their value in order to sell them at their face value to the government, which would pay for them with the fateful loan."

Mosquera also wrote Bolívar that the army was generally favorable to a constitutional monarchy, "and to this opinion have rallied the priests and a few men who hope to be counts and marquises; and these ideas are making headway in the belief that the Holy Alliance will never recognize our independence owing to our Institutions." Concerning the prospect of a monarchy Santander asked Bolívar, "And after your death, who is your successor? Páez? Montilla? Padilla? I want none of them as a crowned Supreme Chief for life." Bolívar had only one candidate to be his successor, but Santander carefully avoided mentioning Sucre.

Bolívar informed Santander that he would abide by the Constitution of Cúcuta and would assume the full powers granted him earlier in order to restore tranquility. He hoped, he added, that in the near future the Bolivarian constitution would be adopted. Santander, fearing that Bolívar planned to create another dictatorship, again advised him not to involve himself with administrative affairs on his return; instead he should lead the army to quell the rebellion in Venezuela. This was a clever device to place Bolívar under Santander's orders, but Bolívar saw through it.

From the outset Bolívar openly favored Páez over Santander despite the fact that Páez had never served him so long and ably. Bolívar considered the Cúcuta constitution too weak, but according to the agreement of 1821 it could not be altered for ten years. He blamed Colombia's ills on inappropriate laws. "We must make a new social contract," he said; "the people must redeem their sovereignty." Santander replied that the Bolivarian constitution would never be popular. Although he had said, "Throw it in the fire if you don't like it — I don't have an

author's vanity," Bolívar now angrily threatened to resign. "I have no desire to preside over Colombia's ob-
sequies," he added.

It was mid-November when Bolívar reached Bogotá,
exhausted from the long journey, and in ill health. He
was not the same Bolívar who had eagerly departed for
the southern conquests five years earlier, but he had been
warmly received in Quito, Pasto, and Popayán, giving
him the false hope that his mere presence could still solve
all problems.

Bolívar announced his arrival in Bogotá with a proclamation that reflected his former ability to move multi-
tudes.

> Colombians! Five years ago I left this capital to march at
> the head of the liberating army, from the banks of the
> Río Cauca to the silvery peaks of Potosí. . . . Your mis-
> fortunes have brought me back to Colombia. I come full
> of zeal to do the will of the people. It will be my code,
> for being sovereign, it is infallible.
>
> The vote of the nation has obliged me to assume the
> supreme command. I utterly detest it, for it is the cause of
> my being accused of having ambitious aims and of at-
> tempting to set up a monarchy. So! Do people think that
> I am so foolish that I am anxious to lower myself? Do
> they not know that the position of Liberator is more sub-
> lime than a throne?

A cold rain fell as Bolívar rode into Bogotá, where he
was greeted by a delegation and a speech referring to
violated laws. Furious, he rose in his stirrups. "This day is
a day set aside for the glory of the army," he said; "talk of
it and not of the broken Constitution." He turned his
horse and left the astonished and offended men standing
in the rain. The streets were decorated in his honor, but
it was a silent welcome, for there were few people to be

seen. From a distance he heard shouts of *"Viva la Constitución,"* and he knew that Santander had planned his reception.

Bolívar rode on through the city almost alone and greeted Santander at the national palace. They agreed to retain the Cúcuta constitution unchanged and that Bolívar would take over the executive authority under the emergency powers granted in Article 128. He soon left for Venezuela, however, delegating his dictatorial powers in Bogotá to Santander and his authority in Ecuador to Briceño. Even before Bolívar set out for Venezuela, Santander had begun a propaganda campaign against him, imputing evil designs to his every action.

Toward Páez Bolívar maintained a friendly and conciliatory attitude, praising him in a letter as one of the pillars of the republic. As the secretary sealed the note, he looked up. "Pearls before swine," Bolívar remarked. The friendly letter failed to reassure Páez, who remained cautious. He announced that Bolívar was coming as a private citizen, which temporarily jolted Bolívar out of his friendly stance. "Your Proclamation says I come as a citizen," he wrote Páez. "What can I do as a citizen? . . . No one has disavowed me; no one has degraded me. Who is going to wrench the reins of command from me? Your friends and yourself? The indignity would be a thousand times worse as ingratitude than as treason. I cannot believe it. . . . There is no legitimate authority in Venezuela but mine, supreme I mean. . . ." Páez assumed that Bolívar was coming to force him to submit to the government of Gran Colombia, and he made plans to fight.

In Puerto Cabello Bolívar's friend Briceño Méndez seized control of the key fortress and declared his support of Bolívar. Arizmendi, Bermúdez, and others were still loyal to the government of Gran Colombia largely because they disliked and distrusted Páez. It seemed that a civil war was in the making, but his failure to recover the Puerto Cabello fortress from Briceño Méndez gave Páez cause for reconsidering his position, and Bolívar's attitude toward him cooled. "It would seem that Providence dooms to perdition my personal enemies," Bolívar reminded him, "whether American or Spanish. . . ." He named a few examples that were well known to Páez; he must make his choice. In the meantime Bolívar began raising an army. Still prepared to fight if he was forced to submit to Santander's authority, Páez sent an emissary with a peaceful message.

Bolívar, who was equally opposed to the government in Bogotá, and who greatly desired to avoid a needless civil war, grasped the opportunity and issued a decree granting general amnesty and confirming Páez as civil and military chief of Venezuela. Páez, equally relieved, responded with a decree acknowledging the Liberator's authority and inviting Venezuelans to welcome him home. In January, 1827, the two men met and embraced so enthusiastically their swords got tangled. Together they entered Caracas, the danger of civil strife past.

In Caracas the editors of public documents informed Bolívar that they intended to withhold from publication some that were unfavorable to his character. "No," he replied, "print them all and let posterity have a fair opportunity of judging me."

Bolívar had effected a reconciliation with Páez, as he desired, but in doing so he had tacitly approved the rebellion against Gran Colombia and had let the rebels off without so much as a slap on the wrist. Páez and his friends were astonished at receiving far more than they had expected or hoped for, and though Páez acknowledged Bolívar's authority, it was a meaningless gesture.

The pact was sealed by a month of festivities, with the usual triumphal arches and maidens in white. Bolívar also had a reunion with his sisters, his old nurse, Hipolita, and friends he had not seen in years. Throughout the celebrations the fiction that Gran Colombia had been saved was kept alive, when in fact it was obvious that Bolívar was rewarding Páez for destroying the union he had created. Bolívar's attitude puzzled many, for he regarded Páez as vain, ignorant, and ambitious, but ever a tool in the hands of others, and the most dangerous man in Gran Colombia.

Bolívar still hoped to create his Federation of the Andes, however, and had concluded that the union created by the Cúcuta constitution was a mistake. Páez had declared the constitution abrogated, and since this fitted with Bolívar's plans, he made no effort to induce him to acknowledge constitutional authority as long as he recognized Bolívar's personal authority as Liberator. "I can't divide the Republic," Bolívar told him, "but I would like to for Venezuela's sake. And this division shall take place when the national assembly meets, if it is the desire of Venezuela." He declared that his only thought now was "the great federation between Peru, Bolivia, and Colombia." He took it for granted that Páez would support him.

What Bolívar had planned was to prevent civil war, to summon the national assembly, to divide Gran Colombia into three states under his Bolivarian constitution, and to cap it all with the Federation of the Andes. His own powers would be preserved as head of the federation for life. "Bolivia has elected Sucre president and has signed an alliance with Peru and Colombia," he said. "Peru has appointed me president and has adopted the Bolivian Constitution. The entire south is willing to ally itself with Colombia, and the Colombian people wish what I wish because they have confidence in me, knowing that I have always had their welfare at heart."

This soliloquy seems to have been to convince himself rather than others, for Bolívar knew that the unity he cherished was fragile, that revolutions would continue, that his was an impossible dream. In a moment of realism he admitted, "They will say of me that I liberated the New World, but they will not say that I have improved the happiness or stability of one single nation in America." Such things appeared to be visionary goals out of reach of all the new nations, yet Bolívar could not admit to himself that anything was beyond his powers.

Even as he dreamed of federation and unity, conspirators in Chuquisaca, Lima, Quito, Bogotá, and even Caracas were working for opposite goals, for it seemed to all that Bolívar had sided with Venezuela against the rest of Gran Colombia. Santander was, with good reason, irate over Bolívar's rewarding Páez instead of reprimanding him for disloyalty, and Santander was a much more intelligent and resourceful foe than Páez. Both Páez and Santander had made substantial contributions to the cause of independence, and both had cooperated with Bolívar, though Páez had done so on his own terms and less effectively than Santander. Without a man of Santander's ability to administer Colombia and provide him with arms and an army — an extraordinary achievement under the circumstances — Bolívar could never have won his triumphs in Peru. To many men his support of the rebellious Páez was incredible.

In January, 1827, the Colombian Third Division Bolívar had left in Lima mutinied under Granadino colonel José Bustamente, who was believed to be Santander's agent, and sent the Venezuelan officers to Callao as prisoners. When Manuela learned of the mutiny she hurried to the barracks in her colonel's uniform and tried to rally the pro-Bolívar troops, but she was arrested and confined in a convent. Santander, on hearing of Bustamente's actions, ordered the bells rung in celebration, an act that was similar to Bolívar's response to Páez, for Bustamente would soon lead Colombian troops in an attempt to seize Ecuador for Peru. The Venezuelan troops were sent on board transports to return to their homeland; Manuela and the Venezuelan officers were also sent by ship to Guayaquil.

With the departure of the Venezuelan troops Bolívar's influence in Peru was at an end, for the Peruvians immediately threw out his cherished constitution and elected Santa Cruz president. Bolívar, knowing that Peru would soon be plunged into anarchy, considered going to Lima to punish those who had betrayed him, but he still had Páez and Santander to consider, and the issues with them could not be postponed.

Colonel Bustamente was offered a substantial reward for detaching Guayaquil from Gran Colombia with what was left of the Third Division. A group of officers living in Guayaquil were still loyal to Bolívar and Gran Colombia, and when they learned of Bustamente's treasonable campaign they prepared defenses and attempted to undermine his control of the Colombian troops he commanded. The troops refused the bait, for they had been convinced it was their duty to destroy Bolívar's dictatorship.

General Juan José Flores, a Venezuelan who had fought for independence, took charge of the campaign against Bustamente, who had already entered Ecuador. Bolívar had praised Flores for his military and political skills and courage, adding, "but his ambition exceeds all his other virtues or defects; it is the motive for all his actions. . . ." Flores, who himself would one day take Ecuador out of Gran Colombia, contacted a number of officers of the Third Division, pointed out that they were aiding a traitor, and, by playing on their patriotism, won them over. They seized Bustamente and his friends and delivered them to Flores.

Guayaquil remained in a state of rebellion, but late in September, 1827, Flores marched into the city and restored

Gran Colombia's authority. To Bolívar this was an encouraging indication that Gran Colombia still supported
him.

Bolívar had remained in Venezuela trying desperately
to revive the defunct administration and to improve the
deplorable economic conditions until June, 1827, when he
set out for Bogotá. As he expected, Caracas was soon again
in chaos. "I never come to the end of my suffering," he
remarked. "What I establish with my hands others trample
underfoot." On his leisurely journey he received com-
plaints of abuses everywhere, all attributed to Santander.
Santander was willing to institute changes and reforms,
but he was deeply offended when Bolívar accused him of
avarice and dishonesty, and he demanded an investigation.
Instead of assuring him that no investigation was necessary, Bolívar unwisely passed the demand to the congress,
where Santander had enemies as well as friends. Congress
appointed a committee to investigate the charges, and
Santander's foes happily used the opportunity to insult
him. Even though the committee never reached a final
decision, the affair ended forever the possibility of reconciliation between Santander and Bolívar.

Until this time the rift between Bolívar and Santander
had been fairly well concealed, and in public Santander
was still outwardly deferential toward the Liberator. In
private he criticized and ridiculed Bolívar, attributing his
every act to his ambition to be king or dictator. And although Bolívar might have been considered liberal in the
early days of the independence struggles, the bitter experi-
ences in Venezuela had convinced him that nothing but
strong, undiluted power could preserve order. All men of
liberal persuasion now encouraged Santander to lead the
opposition to Bolívar, demanded that the union with
Venezuela be dissolved, and used the press to attack both

the lifetime presidency and the idea of a Federation of the Andes.

When Santander learned that Bolívar was returning to Bogotá, he induced the city's garrison to demand that the government support the constitution. Bolívar countered by persuading the garrisons of Maracaibo and Cartagena to demand adoption of the Bolivarian constitution. Alarmed at Bolívar's continued popularity in the army, Santander and his allies took steps they hoped would prevent him from reaching Bogotá, asserting that, like Morillo, he was coming to introduce a reign of terror. If he were coming in peace, they declared, he would not be accompanied by an army.

Santander then wrote Bolívar that the government would not provide subsistence for his troops and they would certainly starve. Bolívar ignored the warning and continued his march, which Santander charged was a violation of the constitution. Bolívar informed the congress that he could not agree to the reduction of his army under pressure — if the congress insisted on reducing it, he would resign the presidency, a threat he had made literally dozens of times before. The troops, he said, were needed because of the Peruvian invasion of Ecuador. Congress was in session when he reached Bogotá. After a cool reception in the city, Bolívar met with the congress and took the oath of office, announcing that he would convoke the National Assembly of Gran Colombia to consider reforms, and calling for the election of delegates in December.

After failing in every effort to prevent Bolívar from taking over the presidency, Santander realized that the Liberator's prestige had survived all efforts to destroy it. He awaited Bolívar's arrival at the presidential palace, where the two men embraced and exchanged flowery but meaningless greetings. At a banquet in Bolívar's honor Soublette's daughter recited a verse and placed a laurel wreath on his head. Bolívar placed it on Santander, saying, "The Vice-President, as the first of the people, deserves this crown." Bolívar was prepared to compromise with Santander; he announced that he had no desire for vengeance and that his enemies who had fled the city on his approach could return in safety. He hoped that he could win them over as he believed he had reconciled Páez, but he was deluding himself in both cases. Santander and his friends were adamant — there would be no compromise with Bolívar.

Santander continued to write "anonymous" articles to spread hatred for Bolívar by means of the press. Dr. Azuero attacked Bolívar even more violently and openly in *El Conductor,* a paper he published. As the vicious campaign against Bolívar intensified, his friends reacted in anger. Vicente Bolívar, a huge llanero descendant of one of Bolívar's former slaves, saw Dr. Azuero walking on the streets of Bogotá and in a towering rage threw him to the ground. He probably would have kicked and trampled Azuero to death if General Córdova had not stopped him.

On his return to Bogotá Bolívar had surprised Santander and others by submitting to constitutional authority. He reorganized all branches of administration and appointed trusted officials. All of his fading hopes now rested on the meeting of the national assembly, which should, he said, decide on the necessary reform of the constitution. He was certain that despite the signs of deterioration and growing rebelliousness in some quarters, Gran Colombia would rise phoenix-like from the ashes, a united and vigorous nation.

Since he based all of his hopes on the "great convention," Bolívar urged that the election be held under tranquil conditions, so that the voters would be able to elect honest and able delegates. He asked all officials to try to pacify the people and factions and to end the warfare in the press, so that the newspapers could devote themselves to calm discussions of the issues.

The press campaign continued unabated despite his request, and passions remained high. Bolívar issued orders prohibiting all officials from campaigning, a restriction that left his party without the help of some of its most influential men, which proved to be a fatal error. Though he hoped to unite all conservative forces of Gran Colombia, Bolívar also abstained from using his position to influence the election, when he should have headed the campaign and worked for the election of a majority of his delegates.

The opposition, led by Santander, was not hampered by any such restrictions or considerations and conducted an active campaign, arousing public fears by asserting that Bolívar planned to establish a brutal military dictatorship. Bolívar expected to lose in Bogotá, where Santander, Azuero, and other sworn enemies won handily. But it was far worse than that, for his foes won a majority of the delegates to the great convention. "This election," he wrote Montilla, "has been carried out in the most infamous and iniquitous manner imaginable. . . . I see no human way of keeping Colombia going; the Convention will do nothing worthwhile and partisanship and civil war will be the outcome of it all." Santander's success in the election enraged him, but it was too late for remedy. Now he could only wait on the sidelines, for he refused to appear at the convention in an effort to influence its decisions.

Exhausted, ill, and despondent, in desperation Bolívar wrote Manuela. "Your love revives a life that is expiring," he said. "I can't live without you. Come. Come to me. Come now."

Manuela, still guarding Bolívar's archives, had reached Quito after a long and difficult journey. She finally received Bolívar's letter and set out on another long and arduous trip, arriving in Bogotá in January, 1828. She found Bolívar at his villa of La Quinta and was shocked at his obvious mental and physical exhaustion. She immediately took charge of him, and he soon showed signs of reviving. But at the age of forty-five years Bolívar was a spent man, prematurely old, and Manuela could not work miracles.

SEVEN

No Liberty under Bolívar

MANUELA LIVED WITH Bolívar at La Quinta or the national palace and openly flaunted their relationship. She appeared in public with him at every opportunity, and she had only contempt for Bogotá's rigid society, which considered it scandalous for the president to live overtly with his mistress. It was not the fact that Bolívar kept a mistress that shocked the social pillars of Bogotá, but that he was not hypocritical and secretive about it as they were about their own private lives. They regarded Manuela as an outsider; in Bogotá all aliens were suspect to begin with, and she took a wicked delight in their pretended horror at her exhibitionist ways, such as riding about dressed as a man. For Bolívar's sake it would have been much better if she had conducted herself discreetly and had made an effort to conform outwardly to local mores. But that was not Manuela's way.

Indispensable though Manuela was to Bolívar, even he was occasionally irritated by her brazen conduct, for he could never predict her next act of folly and he did not enjoy being surprised. She was extremely solicitous of his health and thoroughly devoted and loyal to him, but in a city where he had many astute and unscrupulous enemies, she jeopardized his hope of conciliating or neutralizing some of them, for she knew who they were, and her hatred of them, like her love of Bolívar, was too passionate to be concealed. Polite circles referred to her as "the foreigner," but on other occasions the names they called her were more graphic and even less respectful.

After the disastrous outcome of the election, Bolívar could do nothing but let the great convention destroy the rest of his plans. Frustrated and bitter, alternating between extremes of hope and despair, he wrestled with the temptation to establish a dictatorship and deal with his enemies on his own terms. "The influence of civilization gives our people indigestion," he said in disgust, "so that which should nourish us, ruins us."

Venezuela was still harassed by rapacious bands of presumed royalist guerrillas who were supplied with weapons by Spanish officials in Puerto Rico. Adding to the terror they caused were frequent rumors that Morales was preparing to invade with an army of 12,000 men. Páez pursued and scattered the bands, shooting the leaders and pardoning the followers, but the uprisings were too widespread to be stamped out quickly.

Bolívar, who had no hope of positive results from the meeting of the national assembly at Ocaña, sent O'Leary there to deliver a message to the delegates and to observe and report on the proceedings. He was convinced that his own presence in Venezuela would help restore peace and blunt the expected Spanish invasion, and he probably wanted to forget the Ocaña convention. He issued a decree establishing special tribunals for treason or conspiracy; anyone accused of such acts would be quickly tried and, if found guilty, summarily executed. Instead of relinquishing his powers to Santander as before, Bolívar named Soublette his general secretary and placed Urdaneta in the cabinet — these were men whose loyalty to him was above question. Many interpreted these actions as steps in the process of setting up a dictatorship.

One Bogotá paper printed a diatribe against Bolívar and his "sinister plans," but some of his officers burned the whole edition. The following day the paper appeared with the headline *"El incombustible."* The press campaign continued unabated, and Bolívar could not ignore it. In March he declared that public order was "disturbed," a virtual declaration of martial law. He took drastic steps to eliminate the deficit in the national budget, which also aroused vituperation in the press.

On his way to Venezuela Bolívar learned that Páez had the situation there under control and that the rumored Spanish invasion was a hoax. He did not return to Bogotá, however, for at this time Admiral Padilla, a Granadino supporter of Santander, had rebelled in Cartagena as the national assembly prepared to begin its work in Ocaña. Padilla, a mulatto or zambo, had gained fame by his successes against Spanish warships. A livid scar from his right eye down his cheek gave him a frightening appearance, but he was a respected man with a reputation for being both fair and impulsive.

His rival for power was Bolívar's friend General Mariano Montilla, military commander of Cartagena, who held secret orders from Bolívar to seize control of the whole department in case of emergency. The department of Cartagena included the town of Ocaña, which complicated the matter of Padilla's insurrection. His rash attempt to oust Montilla was apparently inspired by a manifesto Montilla had issued demanding a simple government and restoration of the army's privileges, and implying that the

army would take action if the Ocaña convention failed to
do so. It was signed by many Venezuelan officers, and
apparently originated in Bogotá.

When Padilla declared himself civil and military chief
of Cartagena, and tried to rally the Negroes and *pardos,*
a racial war threatened. Montilla, who was out of the city
at the time, produced his secret orders and assumed command of the department. Padilla's rule lasted only a week,
when he fled to Mompox. There he wrote an explanation
of his conduct to Bolívar and at the same time offered his
services to Bolívar's enemy Dr. Francisco Soto, who was
temporarily presiding at the Ocaña convention.

The national assembly convened in April. Dr. Soto,
whose opening speech clearly reflected his hatred of Bolívar, accepted Padilla's offer. In Ocaña Padilla called on
O'Leary in hope of making peace with Bolívar, but also
met with liberal leaders, presumably to plan a rebellion
against Bolívar should their plans for the convention fail.
O'Leary urged Padilla to write Bolívar, who intended to
name him commandant at Pasto. Instead Padilla returned
secretly to Cartagena, where he was discovered and arrested. Montilla sent him to Bogotá, to be held there for
trial.

Not wanting to appear at Ocaña because he knew that
his motives would be impugned, Bolívar set up headquarters not far away at Bucaramanga, close enough that he
could assume control if necessary. Since he had troops garrisoned in many of the towns of the lower Magdalena
valley, some men accused him of trying indirectly to co-
erce the assembly.

By this time Bolívar had come to rely almost exclusively
on foreign officers as aides, because he was convinced that
there was little likelihood that any of them could be induced to betray him. There were, of course, Venezuelan

and even Granadino officers who were intensely loyal to him, but he needed their services in areas where the use of foreign officers would be resented. As it was, surrounding himself with aliens was another action his enemies used against him. The foreign officers included a Frenchman, Peru de Lacroix, the Scot William Fergusson, the Englishman Belford Hinton Wilson, and O'Leary. In addition to these, other foreigners commanded regiments or held key posts in Bogotá and other cities, including Walter Chitty, Dennis Egan, F. Burdett O'Connor, an Italian named Chassebrune, and the Swede Adlercreutz. Fergusson, at Bolívar's request, maintained a friendly and presumably private correspondence with all of the high-ranking Colombian officers. Bolívar read the letters Fergusson received and suggested replies.

The convention elected as president José María Castillo y Rada, which was a victory of sorts for Bolívar. The tone of the message Bolívar had sent by O'Leary was bitter, and although it did not mention Santander by name there was no question as to whom Bolívar held responsible for misdirecting the government. Congress had usurped all power, the message continued, but the poorly organized government and incoherent laws had led to the decline of agriculture and the disintegration of the army. "We have made the legislative the only sovereign power instead of just a limb of it," he wrote. Only a strong government could restore order. "Without force there is no virtue; without virtue the state dies. Anarchy destroys freedom, but unity preserves it. Give us inexorable laws."

Bolívar's message was delivered to men whose distrust of him was only increased by it. Santander's partisans had tried to prevent the reading of Bolívar's message, but they had little to fear from it. The early sessions were deluged by petitions from city and provincial officials as well as from the military, requesting political reforms as suggested by Bolívar. Convinced that these were all written at Bolívar's request, Santander and his followers ignored them.

Observers recognized from the outset that the Ocaña convention was a deadly duel between the partisans of Bolívar and Santander. Bolívar had relied heavily on effective support from the Venezuelan deputies, but Santander had maneuvered Dr. Peña's ouster on the grounds that he had not been cleared of a charge of embezzlement. "It is strange," Bolívar wrote Briceño Méndez, "that Peña's behavior should be sat on by high criminals of State and by illustrious thieves who have ruined the Treasury of the Republic." O'Leary informed Bolívar that the principal leaders of his party, José María Castillo and Joaquín Mosquera, were not capable of leading — Castillo was too delicate, Mosquera too arrogant. "They were," he said, "powerless in an assembly composed mostly of men dull, foolish, ignorant and blinded by their passions; they can do nothing against the plebeian insolence of Santander, the shamelessness of Soto, the impudence of Gómez, the insanity of Luis Vargas Tejada, and the wickedness of Azuero."

Bolívar sent an aide to Herrera with the suggestion that Colombia be broken up into its component republics, and that he would withdraw completely from public life. His friends assured him that this proposal had the desired effect — when they were sure they had a majority they would invite him to come to Ocaña.

Reform of the constitution was the only item on the agenda, but the convention could not agree on it, so diametrically opposed were the two sides. Castillo wrote Bolívar, "We shall do nothing that is not useful; failing which, we shall go into recess and leave reforms in suspense; and if not even this can be obtained, we shall leave, denouncing the authors of the evil to public execration."

Pleased with Castillo's report, Bolívar waited hopefully at Bucaramanga for an invitation to appear at Ocaña. "Let our friends be united; let them order me to save the Republic and I shall save the whole of America; let them ask me to drive out anarchy, and not even its memory shall remain," Bolívar replied in a burst of enthusiasm. The motion to invite him to Ocaña, however, was defeated because a number of voters reneged on their promises. Bolívar tried to conceal his disappointment by saying that his friends had not thought that "had I gone to Ocaña, the Convention Hall might have been for me what the Capitol was for Caesar; not that I believe Santander, Azuero and Soto would have brandished the daggers . . . but they would have found one or more murderers to take on the affair."

A committee of both parties was appointed to work out the revision of the constitution. Each side presented its own proposal; the assembly unwisely voted to consider both versions at the same time, which was an invitation to mayhem owing to the volatile emotions of the delegates. Their tempers mounted dangerously, and the debate turned into the shouting of insults. Any chance for a compromise was swept away in a flood of oaths, while Bolívar waited, impatient as ever, for news of positive results. The only victory his partisans could claim, however, was the defeat of the Venezuelan deputies' motion to dissolve Gran Colombia's unity into a loose federation.

Torn between the desire to go to Ocaña and reluctance to expose himself to more insults and calumnies, Bolívar sent aides for news and wrote letters by the dozen. He was convinced that the assembly would insist on his presence, but no invitation came. Santander, who was well aware of Bolívar's charismatic personality, knew that if he appeared in person the delegates could not help but admire him. Only in his absence was it possible to maintain a feeling of hatred for him. Santander himself had felt his anger vanish when he confronted Bolívar, and he knew that the other delegates would also melt and lose their determination if Bolívar spoke to them. He had to prevent that at all costs.

Frustrated and tormented, Bolívar withdrew to his room alone whenever he received unfavorable reports from Ocaña. Much of the time he was sunk in black moods of depression, and although O'Leary had called him a thorough atheist, he now turned to the Church for comfort. To the Ecuadorian poet José Joaquín Olmedo he somberly declared: "I have returned to my old position of being a poor devil. My whole taste has become common, averse to power and glory. . . . Yes, my dear friend, I have been converted to the ways of heaven . . . it is time for other heroes to take the stage and play their roles, because my part is over. You know that fortune, like any female, loves change, and since my mistress is tired of me, I myself repent of her." Bolívar, however, had no intention of making way for other heroes.

News of the accusations of Santander, Azuero, Soto, and others that his every action, even his desire to preserve Gran Colombia, was motivated by personal ambition wounded Bolívar more deeply than ever. "What do I need Colombia for?" he asked bitterly. "Even her ruins will testify to my glory. The Colombians will appear before the eyes of posterity covered with ignominy, not I. . . . The wretched creatures! Even the air they breathe they owe to me — and they dare suspect me!"

In a misguided attempt to sway the assembly Bolívar spread the rumor that the army would not accept Santander's program even if he were to have his way at Ocaña. Feeling that his life was in danger, Santander now insisted on protection, then requested his passport. "General Santander asks me for guarantees and even a passport," Bolívar wrote O'Leary; "I shall not fail to seize this opportunity to make him realize his misery." Instead of grasping the opportunity to get Santander out of the country, Bolívar preferred to let him know who held the real power by denying his request.

From Ocaña Briceño Méndez wrote that the money from Barinas had arrived and would be distributed among delegates from Venezuela and the south, since they were the neediest and "because these are the delegations on which we rely for a withdrawal, and they would not be able to do so if they lacked the means." Santander, he said, was thinking of keeping them there by force, "but we shall fight if need be."

In June, when it became obvious that Santander's constitution would be approved, Bolívar's partisans withdrew from Ocaña before a vote could be taken, leaving a bare quorum. When one more delegate was persuaded to depart, the great convention ended.

The Constitution of Cúcuta was defunct, but nothing had been created to replace it. Santander and his partisans remained at Ocaña, apparently planning a coup. Some of them angrily demanded Bolívar's death.

Aware of events at Ocaña, Bolívar warned his friends in Bogotá to be ready for trouble. Pedro Alcántara Herrán, governor of Cundinamarca, called a meeting of citizens at the customs house to consider rejecting any decision made at Ocaña and granting full power to Bolívar. General Córdova, assistant chief of staff, arrived at the meeting and sat quietly while two speakers excoriated Bolívar. When Dr. Juan Vargas began a third tirade against Bolívar, Córdova arose and announced that he would not allow anyone to attack Bolívar in his presence. There was no need for any more discussion; all that remained was to confer full power on Bolívar.

The meeting quickly voted to cancel the commissions of

the Bogotá delegates and to confer all power on Bolívar, and the act was signed "by the servile and timid." The council of ministers approved the decision, and many cities that received assurances that Bolívar would accept the "difficult and delicate mission" also supported the arbitrary action. The council forwarded it to Bolívar, hoping it would "not be disapproved by the Liberator and will at least deserve his indulgence." Bolívar was already on his way to Bogotá when he received the invitation to assume dictatorial powers. "Now the bull is out," he remarked; and José Manuel Restrepo wrote Montilla, "The Liberator is very pleased with the *pronunciamiento* of the capital." José Rafael Arboleda wrote Bolívar frankly: "I must not deceive you; everything is not due to conviction and enthusiasm . . . nevertheless, everybody has bowed down." In Popayán Mosquera "thought it best to keep the troops ready and armed in the barracks in case the coup went awry." And from Caracas Soublette wrote, "It seems to me that the country in general has bowed rather to the influence of circumstances than to conviction. The coldness one perceives and the general isolation observed seem to me signs of discontent."

In his delight at being called on to save the republic, Bolívar ignored these warnings from trusted friends. He reached Bogotá in mid-June and assumed power. "The whole nation recognizes my authority," he said. He increased the size of the army, further damaging the nation that was already suffering from the economic dislocation caused by the war. Although Bolívar did not admit it even to himself, his precious authority, in the last analysis, rested on a group of Venezuelan officers such as Urdaneta, Mariño, Soublette, Arizmendi, and Córdova, and Europeans such as O'Leary, rather than on popular consent. Bolívar abolished the office of vice-president, which eliminated Santander.

There were the usual festivities and celebrations by those who would please Bolívar, even while conspiracies were being hatched by those who would kill him. At one banquet Bolívar toasted Colombia: "The good of the republic does not consist in hateful dictatorship. . . . Dictatorship is glorious when it seals the abyss of revolution, but woe to a people that accustoms itself to live under dictatorial rule." Bolívar wanted badly to convince himself that he ruled with the consent of all — "For I do not want to rule against the will of the people." The title he gave himself was not "Dictator" but "President-Liberator."

Colombians in general hated the dictatorship whether or not they hated Bolívar as well. They were outraged at having a military dictatorship, especially since most of the officers were aliens. And the people of Bogotá despised Manuela passionately.

She had learned no tact and cared nothing at all about the gossips. On one occasion she was having a party when someone suggested that it would be a jolly idea to execute Santander in effigy. An effigy of him was hastily made, and a sign saying "Francisco de Paula Santander dies for treason" was pinned to it. She ordered a detachment of Grenadiers under an Irishman named Crofton to serve as the firing squad, and they riddled the effigy with musket balls.

General Córdova protested to Bolívar, who was furious when he learned of the incident. He was well aware of his friend's fanaticism, he admitted to Córdova, and he had tried repeatedly to break with her. He promised to discipline Crofton and to send Manuela away. He did not keep his promise concerning Manuela, which in one way proved fortunate for him. And Crofton not only remained commandant of cavalry but was promoted as well.

Santander returned to Bogotá and became leader of a conspiracy against Bolívar, a group calling itself the Philological Society, whose motto was There Is No Liberty as

Long as the Liberator Lives. The conspirators were a strange mixture of Venezuelan and Colombian officers, French adventurers, and cuckolded husbands. Venezuelan Major Pedro Carujo and the Frenchman Augustus Horment, believed to be a Spanish agent, were apparently the principal organizers. Some of the civilians, such as Mariano Ospina, simply hated dictatorship. Others, like Florentín González, nursed personal grudges against Bolívar for seducing their wives in times past. It was necessary, they knew, to seize Bolívar and his ministers at the same moment, and they planned to arrest them en masse during the celebrations on Saint Simón's Day in October. It was well known that Bolívar considered himself invulnerable and always appeared in public without sidearms or bodyguard. He could not imagine that anyone would harm the Liberator.

The conspirators changed plans, deciding to murder Bolívar during the masked ball on August 10, the anniversary of the battle of Boyacá. Manuela apparently was warned that an attempt would be made on Bolívar's life that night, and he, too, must have had some inkling of a plot. Manuela appeared at the ball wearing a mask, but soon removed it. Ostensibly annoyed at her prank, Bolívar left the ball early and thereby saved his life.

Santander had been away from Bogotá at the time. Warned of plots against him and of the danger of allowing Santander to remain in Bogotá, Bolívar on September 5 announced that "Santander will leave the country one way or another," then named him minister to Washington. After hesitating, Santander accepted the appointment, asking that Vargas Tejada be assigned as secretary to the legation. Vargas Tejada's home was the conspirators' meeting place. They informed Santander that they planned to kill Bolívar on September 20. He objected; for his own safety he wanted them to wait until he was on his way to Washington. His leadership of the opposition to Bolívar was too well known for him to escape being implicated in Bolívar's murder. The conspirators agreed to postpone the assassination until October 28, Saint Simón's Day.

Because of the drunken revelations of one of the conspirators, a Captain Triana, the others had to act precipitously on the night of September 25. Triana returned to the artillery barracks in an intoxicated condition and began cursing Bolívar, shouting that tyranny would be drowned in blood. To a lieutenant named Salazar he exclaimed that he was a mason and that he and others meant to do in "that old man Bolívar."

Salazar reported the incident to Colonel Ramón Guerra, chief of staff of the Bogotá garrison, who received an order to arrest Triana and hold him for prosecution. Guerra was also one of the conspirators, and he warned the others that since the plot was now known, their only hope for survival was to strike that very night. He sent Major Carujo to warn the others and to summon them to a meeting at Vargas Tejada's home at 7:30 P.M. At 10:00 P.M. more than 100 conspirators, civilians and officers, were sent to the artillery barracks to arm themselves and prepare for action. They divided into three groups: the first was to seize or kill Bolívar; the second was to seize the artillery barracks; the third was to be held in reserve, ready for any unexpected eventuality. Many of the conspirators lost their ardor and quietly disappeared before reaching the artillery barracks.

At midnight ten civilians under Horment and sixteen privates under Major Carujo entered the San Carlos palace and killed three sentries. Earlier in the evening Bolívar, who was ill, had sent for Manuela. She had a pain in her face and did not go until she received a second message, in which he said that she was less ill than he and should come to him. The streets were wet, so she put on a pair of shoes over her slippers. When she arrived Bolívar told her of Triana's arrest and that a revolution was coming, but he thought the immediate threat was over.

As the conspirators entered the palace carrying torches, two of Bolívar's dogs began barking and Manuela heard strange voices. She awakened Bolívar, who seized a pistol and sword and prepared to meet them. Manuela made him dress and slip out the window, while the assassins hammered on the door. Bolívar's boots were out for cleaning, so he wore Manuela's shoes.

After Bolívar had dropped to the ground, Manuela opened the door to stall the assassins while he made his escape. "Where is Bolívar?" they demanded.

"At the sitting of the Council," she replied. They saw the open window. "He has fled!" one of the men exclaimed. "No, I opened it to see what the noise was about," Manuela assured them. They doubted her word, but frantically searched the palace, for if they failed to find Bolívar they would surely face a firing squad. As their panic mounted, one of the soldiers tried to kill Manuela. Horment stopped him. "We're not here to murder women," he said.

Hearing Bolívar's Scottish aide Fergusson approaching the palace on the run, Manuela called to him from the window not to enter. He would die like a soldier, Fergusson replied, and entered the palace. Major Carujo killed him with a pistol shot. One of the conspirators then beat Manuela with the flat of a sword blade, injuring her so severely she was confined to bed for nearly three weeks. Then the terrified men fled, not knowing which way to turn.

Urdaneta, Herrán, and others arrived, all asking anxiously, "And where is he gone?" Bolívar had met one of his servants, and together they ran to the bridge of San Agustín. Hearing shouts and seeing soldiers approaching, they hid waist-deep in the murky water under the bridge for three hours, listening to shouting and gunfire and cavalry horses galloping about. Finally they heard soldiers shouting vivas for Bolívar. Suspecting it might be a trap, Bolívar sent his servant to check; then wet and shivering, he accompanied the troops to the barracks.

The attempt to seize the artillery barracks had also failed, for although the conspirators were able to free Admiral Padilla, the regiments remained loyal to Bolívar. Urdaneta immediately took charge and ordered the conspirators arrested. By dawn the rebellion had been completely crushed and many of the rebels were in custody.

While Horment's party was trying to assassinate Bolívar, a party of artillerymen had climbed over the wall between their barracks and the building in which Padilla was imprisoned under the custody of Colonel José Bolívar, Simón's nephew. Padilla heard the colonel shout, "General, I'm being killed!" He tried to find refuge behind Padilla, while an officer and some soldiers shot him. At this time the loyal Vargas battalion advanced on the rebels, who disappeared, leaving Padilla alone with the dead colonel. Although Padilla was innocent of Colonel Bolívar's death, it was an awkward situation for him, for he was already in deep trouble. He hid during the night, and in the morning went to the central plaza, to Bolívar and the troops. He embraced Bolívar and congratulated him on his escape.

Santander had spent the night at his sister's home, where she always had a bed ready for him. He remained there until General José María Ortega, accompanied by a body of troops, rapped on his window and told him what had happened. Santander accompanied Ortega to the central plaza. When he tried to congratulate Bolívar on his fortunate escape, he was rebuffed.

Bolívar had gone to the barracks to change into a dry uniform, and then rode to the plaza, where the entire garrison received him with enthusiastic shouts. "Do you want to kill me with joy when I am on the point of dying with grief?" he asked them hoarsely. In a barely audible voice he thanked them for their loyalty.

Returning to the San Carlos palace, Bolívar found Manuela ill with a high fever. "This night you have been the liberatress of the Liberator," he told her. Then, as the captured conspirators were brought to the palace, he listened while their depositions were taken. Bolívar had to restrain Colonel Crofton, who started to strangle Horment, then he ordered that the young Frenchman be given dry clothing. "And this is the man you would kill!" General José (Pepe) Paris exclaimed. "Not the man, but his system," Horment replied.

Bolívar decided to proclaim general amnesty and then resign, for he felt that his cherished glory had been destroyed beyond repair. If the people could not understand his efforts to save them, he had no other course left. He sent for José María del Castillo and asked him to assemble the council so he could submit his resignation. Castillo should also summon the congress immediately, draw up a decree pardoning all of the conspirators, and prepare for Bolívar's departure from Colombia. In his grief he did not want to know who the other conspirators were. Castillo listened with folded arms and a pained expression. Gently he urged Bolívar to withdraw to La Quinta as a private citizen, suggesting that if he left the country at this time he would reinforce the opinion that opposition to him was widespread. Wearily Bolívar assented.

Urdaneta, Córdova, and dozens of other officers visited Bolívar, pointing out to him in strong terms that if he withdrew they would all be ruined. The army had demonstrated its deep loyalty to him, and he should not abandon it now. The conspiracy, they said, should be completely stamped out and the conspirators punished. His resignation would give tacit approval to the attempted murder. Bolívar listened and nodded in agreement. He sent word to Castillo canceling his previous orders.

Declaring himself dictator, Bolívar placed Urdaneta in charge of the investigation. He set up a special court of high-ranking officers and a few civilians to try the accused. Death sentences levied on Horment and a dozen others were quickly carried out. Padilla, who had no part in the conspiracy, was also executed. The court was divided over Ramón Guerra, who had spent all of September 25 at Castillo's home, and gave him thirty years in prison. Bolívar overruled the court and ordered Guerra executed. The search for others continued, spurred on by Bolívar himself. Young Jóse Celestino Azuero, son of Bolívar's archenemy, was captured and executed. The senior Azuero was sent into exile.

Santander went to Urdaneta during the night to ask his advice. Urdaneta stalled, and the next day ordered him arrested. Bolívar and others were convinced that Santander had been the driving force behind the would-be assassins. He was charged with participation in the assassination attempt, but denied being an accomplice. He did admit, however, that he had been aware of the plot and had given the conspirators advice when they approached him. Carujo had saved his life by testifying against others, especially Santander, but he failed to give conclusive proof of Santander's guilt. He was later exiled permanently.

Urdaneta, nevertheless, sentenced Santander to die. Bolívar submitted the verdict to the council of ministers, who agreed that the sentence was justified but protested that executing Santander would cause a violent reaction. Bolívar had overruled the court in the case of Ramón Guerra, but he bowed to the council in the case of Santander. A great many people visited Santander during the few days he was given to set his affairs in order — mainly women whose husbands were afraid of arousing Bolívar's wrath by calling on Santander themselves. British Consul James Henderson estimated that all but a few of the "respectable part of the inhabitants" called on him or sent him some sign of their respect. The archbishop and the clergy were outspoken in his defense. Had the death sentence been carried out a large group of priests and women were determined to shield Santander from the firing squad.

Bolívar was angry at the council's suggestion, but agreed to commute the sentence to exile. To Páez, he complained, "My life remains in the air with this reprieve, and that of Colombia is lost forever. I regret the deaths of Piar, Padilla and the rest who have perished for the same cause." Bolívar seemed to be the overwhelming victor of the assassination attempt, but he later admitted, "It was our ruin that we did not come to terms with Santander." In the end Santander would serve as Colombia's president when Bolívar was gone from the scene.

Santander was escorted to Cartagena, to be held in Bocachica castle in the harbor until allowed to sail abroad. The congressmen known to be inimical to Bolívar were sent away, but the conspirators who had fled to safety were later granted amnesty. The Masonic lodges, which had been centers of liberal dissent, were closed, and education was reorganized to eliminate its liberal aspects. More and more Bolívar, who had once scornfully referred to an oration by a priest as "a flood of words over a desert of thought," turned to the clergy for help in keeping the people peaceful.

The night affair of September 25 was the cruelest blow Bolívar had received during his hectic life, and he suffered the more because he was mentally and physically worn out. All of his dreams of glory were gone — "They have destroyed my heart," he admitted. The physical decline that had appeared during his stay in Peru was steadily advancing, and sickness of body, together with the obvious fact that his years of effort and sacrifice had been in vain, deepened his depression. He could bear no more ingratitude, he declared, "For I am not a saint, and I have no desire to suffer martyrdom."

British Consul Henderson, an admirer of Bolívar, wrote his government concerning the Liberator.

> It cannot be denied that he is deficient of practical knowledge in matters of legislation, and I am besides fearful that he will not have the energy to maintain the position he has taken. . . . The opinion that this country cannot prosper without a constitutional monarchy gains ground: it would not be surprising if . . . some proposition were made to the Liberator to look for a successor in a European Catholic Prince. . . . One complaint against the government of General Bolívar is that justice is not fairly administered, as the adherents of the Liberator are always allowed to escape.

Talk of establishing a constitutional monarchy was renewed by Bolívar's friends. At a meeting of the council of ministers, Bolívar announced his desire to call the national assembly into session, to report on his administration, surrender his authority, and ask it to prepare a constitution. Restrepo and others opposed the proposal, declaring that the nation, "by a unanimous and solemn decision," had granted him unlimited powers. Bolívar's proposal was rejected, probably as he had intended it would be. It was expected that the army and the cities would request him to grant the country a constitution without calling a convention. The result would be, some predicted, a constitutional monarchy, although it seems more likely that Bolívar would have imposed his own favorite constitution — the one he had written for Bolivia.

EIGHT

Bolívar's War with Peru

IN BOLIVIA SUCRE governed with integrity and justice, qualities which set him apart from those around him and made him appear weak. A Captain Valentín Matos tried to assassinate him and was sentenced to death. Owing to the pleas of the captain's mother, and recalling his regret over the hasty execution of Echeverría, Sucre granted Matos a reprieve and gave him 200 pesos out of his own pocket, a gesture that confirmed suspicions of his weakness.

Sucre retained a part of the Colombian army, and the arrogant attitude of some of the officers led to resentment. Simón Rodríguez also caused such widespread opposition Sucre finally had to dismiss him.

Peruvians had not abandoned their desire to annex Bolivia as well as Ecuador. Generals Agustín Gamarra and Santa Cruz, both natives of Upper Peru, were restless and ambitious, and Gamarra marched toward the Bolivian border with Peruvian troops. Gamarra hated Bolívar with the bitterness of a cuckolded husband and was eager to avenge his wounded pride against anyone close to Bolívar. Through agents he engineered a rebellion in Bolivia in

December, 1827, but Sucre quickly restored order. He tried to persuade Gamarra that neither he nor Bolívar was his enemy, and Gamarra pretended to be convinced.

In April, 1828, the garrison at Chuquisaca, shouting vivas for Gamarra, mutinied while Sucre was passing through the city. He rode at once to the barracks, where he met a volley of musket fire that tore his clothing and shattered his arm. Bolivian officials invited Gamarra to cross the border, presumably to protect Sucre. He marched in and forced an agreement on them, which they were secretly eager to sign, agreeing to expel all foreigners, meaning Colombians, from the country. Sucre courageously refused to resign until the congress met in August; he left immediately for Quito.

Bolívar regarded the Bolivians' treatment of Sucre as an offense against Colombia, and he was equally irritated by the hostile attitude of Peruvians. The Peruvian government sent as minister to Bogotá José de Villa, formerly the private secretary of General Juan Berindoaga, who had gone over to the royalists and had been executed on Bolívar's orders after Callao surrendered. Villa carried funds to use in arranging for the assassination of Bolívar and immediately made contact with José María Obando and other members of the opposition. Bolívar refused to see him unless Peru reimbursed Colombia for the expenses of the liberating expeditions as agreed. Villa repudiated the treaties and Peru's debt.

In response Bolívar published a proclamation in which he urged Colombians of the south to arm and prepare for conflict. "My presence among you," he concluded, "will be the signal for war." He sent O'Leary to Lima to negotiate a compromise or, at worst, to gain time while Bolívar raised an army. The Peruvian government refused to give O'Leary a guarantee of safe conduct, so he did not reach Lima. He wrote Bolívar from Quito that everyone, including the Peruvians, was opposed to the war; since this was unwelcome news, Bolívar ignored it.

Peruvian President José de la Mar responded to Bolívar's provocative proclamation with a similar broadside of his own in which he attacked both Bolívar and Sucre. Sucre reached Guayaquil in September and spent a day with O'Leary discussing the impending war that both of them dreaded as senseless and wasteful. Sucre, whose arm was still paralyzed from its wound, was willing to serve Bolívar, though he was most anxious to retire completely from public life. If he were to serve, he said, he wanted to know the reasons for doing whatever he was asked to do.

In October Peruvian warships blockaded Guayaquil and Colombia's Pacific coast ports, while La Mar approached the Ecuadorian border with 5,000 men. Bolívar named Sucre his personal representative, and he reluctantly assumed command of the southern operations, much to the irritation of the ambitious Flores. At the same time Sucre politely informed Bolívar, "The declaration of war without control of the sea in the Pacific was premature." The Peruvian squadron attacked Guayaquil unsuccessfully and lost indispensable Admiral Guise in the process. Without him the Peruvian fleet was no longer a serious threat.

At Ocaña a plan for rebellions in the various provinces had been agreed on, and in the Cauca valley Colonel José María Obando and Lieutenant Colonel José Hilario López led an uprising. They looted and murdered for a month, then went to Pasto, where they recruited 3,000 Indians by assuring them they were fighting for king and religion. From Pasto Obando wrote La Mar, offering to cooperate with him, saying with reference to Bolívar, "The republicans of Colombia are resolved to compromise only with his ashes."

On learning of the revolt Bolívar sent General Córdova to prevent the rebels from joining forces with La Mar.

Bolívar and Córdova had been, at the time, studying the possibility of a canal across Panama, a project they were never able to resume. Soon afterward Bolívar turned over administrative responsibilities to the council of ministers and proceeded south, though he was so weak he could not ride more than two hours at a time without resting. Only his grim determination to thrash Peru and enter Lima in triumph kept him going.

In February Sucre met La Mar's army on the plain of Tarqui, and in a battle of 1,500 Colombians against 5,000 Peruvians, Sucre outmaneuvered La Mar and O'Leary led a cavalry charge that decided the outcome of the battle. Thoroughly routed, La Mar had no choice but to accept Sucre's generous terms.

Bolívar was hurrying south so as not to miss out on any important action, whether of peace or war. He found Obando in Pasto blocking his path. Because of Obando's strong position, Bolívar, who was unaware that La Mar had already been defeated, was obliged to negotiate. He agreed to promote Obando to general and to exempt Pasteños from military service for a year. It was humiliating for Bolívar, for if he had not been in such a hurry he could have waited for troops from Quito to attack Obando from the rear, and dealt with him as he deserved. When the negotiations were concluded Bolívar rode on toward Pasto, meeting Obando on the way. Almost alone he trusted his life to Obando for half a day until Córdova arrived with his troops.

All of Bolívar's sacrifices on this occasion were vain and unnecessary. Córdova noted, "When H. E. heard in Pasto of the preliminary peace entered into by General Sucre, he was much annoyed." Bolívar itched for action against the Peruvians, and he preferred to humiliate them for what he regarded as their treachery to him and to Sucre. If there was to be peace, it must be on his terms. In this campaign Bolívar was seeking vengeance, not "glory."

Córdova, like Sucre, was much opposed to waging an offensive war against Peru, and he was one of the few officers who was also frank with the Liberator. Bolívar had, in fact, assured him that he would dismiss Crofton and Manuela after the effigy affair, and he was far from grateful when Córdova pointed out that he had promoted Crofton instead of cashiering him and had not sent Manuela away. An unfortunate coolness developed between Bolívar and Córdova, and Mosquera, who hated Córdova for tactlessly telling him he had made a mess of the Popayán campaign against Obando, skillfully widened the breach by innuendo concerning Córdova's loyalty to Bolívar.

Córdova was becoming disillusioned with Bolívar, who had once been his idol. As he wrote to British Consul Henderson, whose daughter, Fanny, Córdova was wooing, "The nation has no constitutional government, it is subject to the will of one man, and of a man who already may be said to be in a declining state of health."

Early in April, 1829, Bolívar reached Quito, where he had an emotional reunion with Sucre — so emotional, in fact, that Bolívar was unable to speak. Sucre, who had married the Marquesa de Solanda by proxy the day he resigned his command in Bolivia, had his home in Quito, and he wanted badly to live in quiet as a civilian. Because of his thoroughly honest nature and sense of integrity, Sucre was unable to conceal the truth from Bolívar. On one occasion in Quito he handed Bolívar a request from Santander to be released from the castle in Bocachica.

Bolívar refused to take the petition from Sucre's hand. Sucre insisted that he consider it like any other petition, and Bolívar finally yielded. Sucre was equally frank in pointing out how foolish and undesirable a war with Peru would be, which was certainly not what Bolívar wanted to hear. Because he yearned for war rather than peace, Bolívar considered the terms Sucre had given Peru too generous, letting the Peruvians off without the punishment he felt they richly deserved. All was not lost, however, for Bolívar was sure that the Peruvians would violate the terms of the convention, which would be excuse enough to invade.

Because of Sucre's opposition to war with Peru, Bolívar leaned more heavily on Flores, who was still annoyed that Bolívar had placed Sucre over him. Flores was, however, too discreet to voice any opposition to Bolívar's plans. Forgetting his earlier comments regarding Flores's unbounded ambition, Bolívar now frequently referred to him as a "great man."

Bolívar opened communications with General Gamarra, who saw an opportunity to even the score with both Bolívar and La Mar by egging them on to destroy one another. La Mar helped Gamarra's cause by asking for men and money to continue the war, and by ordering the Peruvian troops in Guayaquil not to surrender the port to Colombia. Bolívar, who was watching eagerly for such a violation of the agreement, wrote Urdaneta, "They wrote to me from Lima that if I come nearer to Peru, my return there will be like that of Napoleon to France." Ever an admirer of Napoleon, Bolívar increasingly saw parallels in their careers, which was one reason many men were certain that he would ultimately claim a crown.

In his eagerness to shed Peruvian blood, Bolívar planned a forced march to Guayaquil in the rainy season. Sucre and Córdova were both appalled at the idea, and warned Bolívar that marching against Guayaquil in that season would be disastrous to the troops. To Córdova Bolívar admitted that "many deaths will occur before the city is taken, owing both to the climate and to the war." He ordered Córdova and Mosquera to Quito, then named the latter chief of staff, a post which should have been assigned to Córdova on the basis of military experience and ability. He was a veteran and one of the principal heroes of Ayacucho, while Mosquera had bungled his only campaign.

Greatly irritated at this intentional affront, Córdova returned to Popayán and opened communications with the liberal opposition. He was convinced that Bolívar was physically and mentally unfit for rule, and planned to depose him before he caused a disaster to the exhausted country, which simply could not support the army he had raised.

Talk of establishing a monarchy was revived, and Sucre and others feared that the army might simply proclaim Bolívar emperor. Candid as ever, Sucre suggested to Bolívar that he retire and invite a British prince to rule Colombia. Henderson reported to his government: "When such generals as Sucre and Córdova begin to see that the policy of General Bolívar is inimical to the interests of the country . . . it is not to be wondered at that much concealed discontent prevails in other quarters. General Bolívar for the last twenty years has governed in South America according to his will, and the idea is current that it will be difficult or impossible for him to conform to any code of laws that does not invest him with a large share of power."

Ignoring the warnings of Córdova and Sucre, Bolívar launched his campaign to retake Guayaquil. Because it had been impossible to equip the troops adequately, many men lacked tents, and a shockingly large number were lost to disease. Although the patriot armies had always lost many more men on long marches than in battles, this was much worse than usual. Córdova requested to be retired from the army.

In Cuenca Bolívar wrote the pamphlet *A View of Spanish America*, in which he stated: "There is neither faith nor trust in America, whether it be among men or among nations. Treaties are mere scraps of paper, constitutions are books, elections are battles, freedom is anarchy, and life is torture. This is our situation, and if we do not change it, it were better that we should die." In his anguish he virtually repudiated all of the sacrifices made for the cause of independence. "We lost our individual guarantees when, in order to obtain them perfect, we sacrificed our blood and our most precious pre-war possessions; and if we turn back our eyes to that time, who can deny that our rights were more respected." He sent copies of the pamphlet to his friends, saying, à la Voltaire, that it was written by "a friar who has a good deal of talent." His purpose, according to Córdova, was to make republican government odious and to make Colombians "on their knees pray of H. E. to place the Crown on his head."

In June Peruvian General Antonio Gutiérrez de la Fuente, who was marching north with a division, toppled La Mar's government and proclaimed himself temporarily Supreme Chief in behalf of Gamarra. He assured Bolívar that Peru would never forget Colombia's services. While La Mar went into exile, Gamarra signed an armistice in which he agreed to return Guayaquil to Colombia. As a result, Bolívar and his ill and exhausted army entered Guayaquil without firing a shot — all of the sufferings and losses of life during the march had been needless.

In Guayaquil Bolívar himself was seriously ill, probably as a result of tuberculosis, which was gradually destroying him. He could not, even under these circumstances, give up his dream of returning to Lima in triumph. He was sure that Gamarra would not last long in power, thinking "that in the end the Peruvians will have to call me." He was resolved not to go to Peru, he said, for he had too much to do in Colombia, and besides, "I have had enough of power" — a statement that did not square with the preceding ones.

Once more Sucre urged caution, writing him that Peruvian General Blas Cerdeña, who had commanded the Peruvian troops in Guayaquil, "tells you that La Fuente, Santa Cruz, and Gamarra are your friends, and I am certain he is somewhat mistaken." Again, when Bolívar talked of resigning, Sucre wrote him:

A time may come to silence your slanderers; but the best action now . . . is to constitute the country and to set its affairs on a stable basis. Nothing else is worthy of you. To retire when the Republic is threatened by so many risks, merely in order to prove your disinterestedness, is a measure foreign to your character; and to be candid, will be looked upon by all the world as a mere trick, so that in the fray of parties, and when a thousand daggers may quarter the fatherland, you might be called back as the savior and conciliator.

On another occasion Sucre chided Bolívar:

I shall always regret that in order to secure this inner peace and this steady progress, you should not have made use of your dictatorial power to grant Colombia a constitution that would have been backed by the army, and which is with us the initiator of tumults against the laws. What the people want is repose and guarantees; for the rest I do not think they would quarrel over principles or political abstractions from which the right of property and of security have suffered so much.

The ailing Bolívar pathetically still hungered for more "glory." When Urdaneta wrote him that people were coming back to him he was thrilled. "More than with any of

your news I am pleased by that which you send me that
the nation gives me back my aura as in the first days of my
glory," he wrote. "May God grant, my friend, that you do
not deceive yourself out of your desire to bring me back
to life with the only element which you know could do it."

Although he talked of sailing for France, Bolívar still
hungered for personal power, a lifelong presidency rather
than a crown. He was warned that anarchy would surely
spread following his departure. He did not, of course,
actually intend to leave, but by nature he needed the reas-
surance that he was indispensable.

A Frenchman, M. Bresson, who came to Bogotá to observe conditions and to look into the possibility of placing
a French prince on a Colombian throne, reported what he
had heard about the Liberator, who was still in the south.

> Bolívar, thirsty for power, works only for himself. Bona-
> parte is his model; war is his element, impatient at every
> contradiction, ardent, impetuous, he has been for so long
> exclusively at the head of affairs, he has, unaided, accom-
> plished such big things, that his confidence in himself
> knows no bounds, and such opposition as is natural under
> a free government appears in his eyes as a kind of mili-
> tary insubordination to be put down forthwith. Every-
> thing around him breathes the spirit of despotism. . . .
> His hypocrisy is as deep as his ambition. He has often
> resigned only in order to be offered power again, to gain
> the glory of refusing it and make his authority thrive on
> the security his simulated moderation had fostered.

This astute observer also reported that Juan García del
Río was promoting the idea of monarchy, with the support
of Urdaneta, Montilla, Sucre, and Flores, although Sucre
had consistently warned Bolívar against accepting a crown.
Bresson added that Bolívar had said he would abide by
whatever decision congress might make.

"Does this mean," Bresson asked rhetorically, "that he would accept the Crown? It is certain that he would first refuse, resist for long, write letters, which would be ostentatiously circulated and published." But, he added, if Bolívar did not check his friends, "he will, in the end, accept the throne which is offered to him." The idea in Bresson's mind was to make sure that his heir and successor was a French prince.

When government officials spoke to him of constitutional monarchy, Bolívar suggested a British protectorate, but it seems clear that he was offering a choice that most men would regard as less desirable than a lifelong presidency or monarchy under Bolívar. "He likes to compare his deeds with those of Alexander, Caesar, and Bonaparte," Bresson remarked,

> and without hesitation, rates himself above them. . . . He thinks very little of Washington, and his aversion for North Americans comes, in part, from their obstinacy in comparing him with this somewhat pale hero of their revolution. Ambition absorbs every other feeling in him: he wants to command, to govern without fetters, constraint or laws; he wants Colombia to be fully his; to be indispensable; and the thought that, when he is gone, all must fall into confusion, does not displease. . . . He will not give up his ambition to rule over Peru and Bolivia. Immense Colombia is too small for him.

After reading letters from Bolívar to Castillo and Urdaneta, Bresson commented, "I deeply regret that General Bolívar is not here. . . . Hitherto, he has played his part before an audience of too poor a moral order and too alien to things of the world. He knows exactly the thoughts and the gestures that will impress them. A European," he boasted, "would see through it easily."

Urdaneta assured Bresson that he "considered himself

in possession of the Liberator's assent for his monarchical plans." He and Castillo pleaded with Bolívar to "conquer what he calls his delicacy and to express himself in positive terms about himself and the French Prince discussed as his successor." Bolívar replied that, under present circumstances, the prince would not be flattered by the offer; the country was not ready for a monarchy. A lifelong president and hereditary senate might create and unite monarchical elements needed to prepare for the future accession of some prince.

Although Bresson found Bolívar incomprehensible, he nevertheless considered him the outstanding man in Spanish America. "This extraordinary man," he wrote, "appears to me under so many different lights that trust and fear follow each other in my mind. . . . It cannot be doubted that his ambition is extreme. . . . He has a blind confidence in his own powers, and yet his actions are hallmarked by indecision and hesitancy. He will stall before his wisest plans for vain personal consideration, for fear of a newspaper article. He seeks power, accepts it, yet wants to come out at the head of those who protest."

Among the generals there were two main groups — those who expected to benefit from a monarchy under Bolívar, and those who were, like Páez, too ambitious or, like Córdova, too dissatisfied to expect anything worthwhile to come from the scheme. But the former were in the majority and kept up their agitation. Even though Bolívar consistently opposed a monarchy, since he did not silence his friends they assumed that this was tacit approval.

Although Sucre remained firmly loyal to Bolívar despite disapproving some of his actions, Bolívar himself drove General Córdova into defecting. He sent a subtly worded letter to a Colonel Jiménez, one of Córdova's subordinates, suggesting that he "use his sword" against any attempt at rebellion by anyone of any rank. Jiménez, who had earned his rank on the battlefield, had never learned to read and had to have the letter read to him. Córdova was informed of the letter, and he clearly understood its implications. Bolívar wrote him a lame and unconvincing explanation, then named him minister of the navy. Since Colombia had no navy, Córdova was far from soothed. Bolívar then named him minister to Holland, but by then it was too late for him to accept a polite form of exile, for he had already issued a manifesto in Medellín. "A holy cause unites us," he declared; "to conquer power in order to put it under the safeguard of the law."

When Urdaneta learned of the revolt he sent O'Leary with a force of picked troops to deal with Córdova, who had only a small and untrained following. At the same time Castillo published another proclamation defending Bolívar against Córdova and his demand for a return to the Cúcuta constitution. O'Leary's detachment frightened off Córdova's subordinates, leaving him virtually defenseless. Córdova fought furiously until he was struck down by musket balls. As he lay helpless from his wounds, the Irishman Rupert Hand found him and killed him. This was the tragic and ignominious end of one of the principal heroes of the patriot victory at Ayacucho.

Bolívar was forced to return to Bogotá and forsake his dream of conquering Peru, but his actions were confusing to those around him. "He seems the prey of a thousand feelings and of a thousand contradictory schemes," Bresson commented. "Everything in him is uncertainty and contradiction. Weakness follows energy, waking up follows sleepiness; one might believe oneself in the presence of the agony of a great soul. A noble, struggling intelligence is becoming extinct; his influence, his popularity, his reputation suffer therefrom. The members of the Government are at a loss what to do next."

The widespread criticism of Bolívar's dictatorship

wounded him as such attacks always did. He was in despair, and his health steadily worsened. "My name already belongs to history," he consoled himself, "and there I shall have justice." At the same time Bolívar had many European admirers. King Bernadotte of Sweden even compared himself to Bolívar. "We both owe our rise to our swords and our merits," he pointed out; "we are both beloved by our people; we are faithful to the cause of liberty, distinguishing ourselves from Napoleon in this matter."

A new separatist movement had appeared in Venezuela, which was still in ruins from the devastating independence wars. Arizmendi controlled the police, which angered Páez, who commanded the army and who was therefore all-powerful. He publicly blamed Bolívar for all of Venezuela's troubles, calling him tyrant and worse. This had been the situation in September, 1829, when Córdova wrote Páez asking him for help.

Bolívar's preoccupation with Córdova's rebellion had given Páez the opportunity to declare Venezuela independent of Gran Colombia. He lashed out against Bolívar's dictatorship and plan to crown himself, a plan which Páez himself had encouraged. Bolívar's friends immediately published his letter to O'Leary in which he declared himself against a monarchy and reiterated his desire to give up all power. The letter did not end the attacks on Bolívar, and the walls of Caracas were plastered with posters condemning him. Páez and Arizmendi remained alert for an opportunity. It came when Bolívar issued a pamphlet saying that local communities should express their views concerning the form of government, constitution, and person who was to be chief executive.

When he received the pamphlet, Páez had a copy sent to every parish with instructions for the people to pass resolutions asking congress to declare Venezuela independent. He then took an oath declaring Venezuela independent of Gran Colombia. Bolívar warned him, "I do not want power, but should anyone seek to wrench it from me by force or intrigue, I shall fight to the bitter end." The Venezuelan congress voted to secede from Gran Colombia, to reject Bolívar's authority, and to grant full civil and military power to Páez. He wrote Bolívar that Venezuela would return to Spanish rule rather than be governed from Bogotá. When he learned of Venezuela's actions, Bolívar commented sadly, "I have lost much with this movement, for I have been deprived of the honor of leaving spontaneously."

In January, 1830, Bolívar was again in Bogotá. Many people were shocked to see how rapidly his health was failing, for he was pale and weak, his eyes dull, and his voice a mere whisper. He yielded to pressure to call for election of a new congress, but he still maintained his authority by his personal magnetism.

Presiding over the opening of congress, Bolívar received military honors as chief of state for the last time. At his request Sucre came out of retirement once more, to serve as president of the congress and, Bolívar hoped, to facilitate Sucre's election as President of the Republic. The Bishop of Santa Marta was elected vice-president of the congress, to demonstrate Bolívar's reliance on the Church. After recommending the establishment of institutions which combined the force of government with the liberty of the people, Bolívar declared, "I withdraw with the utmost confidence in the success of a Congress presided over by the Grand Marshal of Ayacucho [Sucre], the worthiest of all Colombian generals." Urdaneta, who was present, struck his forehead with his hands and "showed the strongest symptoms of agitation and displeasure," said an English observer. Bolívar's remark was an error, a slip of the tongue, for in his prepared speech he had written *"one of the* worthiest [italics added]." But the damage was done, for now Urdaneta, too, had been alienated.

Addressing the congress concerning who should rule the country, Bolívar declared: "I fear with some grounds that my sincerity may be doubted when I speak to you about the magistrate who is to preside over the Republic. . . . Honor debars me from thinking of myself for this appointment. . . . Believe me: a new magistrate has become indispensable for the Republic. . . . You will permit that my last act be to recommend you to protect the holy religion we profess, an abundant spring of heavenly blessings."

In March Bolívar called Urdaneta, Herrán, and others to a meeting in which he proposed to resume authority and declare war on the Venezuelan separatists. Urdaneta, still smarting from Bolívar's praise of Sucre, coldly replied that Venezuela had been independent since 1827, when Bolívar had pardoned Páez. All agreed that the war would be extremely unpopular, for the separation of Venezuela was complete and final, and was accepted by everyone. Bolívar now faced the bitter fact that he could no longer count on the enthusiastic support of his former friends, who seemed to consider him more of a liability than an asset. One even suggested that he retire permanently. The meeting ended with nothing decided except that Gran Colombia was no more.

Despite the warnings of Urdaneta and others, Bolívar went ahead with his preparations for invading Venezuela. He organized two divisions, one under O'Leary, the other commanded by the Swede Adlercreutz. Part of the latter's division mutinied and went over to Páez. Congress, anxious to avoid a war, named Sucre and the Bishop of Santa Marta to negotiate with Páez on the basis of no separation, republican government, and no reprisals. Sucre predicted failure, and, as he expected, the Venezuelan delegates insisted on recognition of Venezuela's independence. On that note the meeting broke up.

Citing ill health, Bolívar resigned, asking congress to appoint his successor. The congress, fearing that anarchy would follow, stalled, saying he could not be replaced until a new constitution had been accepted and new officials elected. Bolívar named pliable General Domingo Caicedo provisional president and retired to a farm in the country to restore his health. He was as ambitious as ever, though his disease-ridden body no longer responded to his powerful will.

A friend who visited Bolívar at this time wrote:

> He walked slowly and with fatigue, and his voice was so low that he had to strain himself to be heard; he would walk by the banks of a brook that winds its way through the picturesque countryside, and with crossed arms stopped to watch the stream, an image of life. "How long" — he said to me — "will this water run before it dissolves itself into the ocean, as man dissolves in the rot of the grave into the earth from which he came? Much of it will evaporate and become subtle, like human glory, renown!" Then, in agony, "My glory! My glory! Why do they wrench it from me? Why do they slander me?"

"I am resolved," Bolívar wrote Mosquera, "to leave Colombia to die of sadness and poverty in some foreign land. Oh, my friend, my grief has no measure, for slander stifles me like Laocoön's serpents!"

Because Castillo and Urdaneta, once among his most dedicated supporters, both urged him to accept the separation of Venezuela and not to return to the presidency of Colombia, Bolívar angrily accused them of trying to gain the presidency and vice-presidency for themselves. He was more isolated than ever, yet he could not bring himself to accept the inevitable and retire.

Caicedo freed the press from restrictions Bolívar had imposed on it in 1828, and it was soon attacking Bolívar for his "excessive desire to please the military," especially when he was contending with Santander. Bolívar still planned to get himself elected president with Caicedo as vice-president. He sent for Urdaneta, who advised him bluntly to leave the country. Rumors Bolívar would be leaving caused much anxiety among foreigners in Bogotá, and the ministers of Brazil and the United States both urged him to remain. They, like many thoughtful Colombians, feared an outbreak of anarchy would follow his departure. Bolívar assured them privately that he would accept the presidency, but publicly declared that he would refuse it.

William Turner, British minister in Bogotá, commented concerning Bolívar: "The dejection of his mind is evident in his countenance, and has so serious an effect on his health that unless a beneficial change ensue, Colombia may ere long have to mourn the loss of the only one of her citizens who is capable of preserving her tranquility or ameliorating her condition."

While congress was completing its work on the new constitution and preparing to hold elections, García del Río led Bolívar's partisans. For the third time Bolívar called a meeting of ministers and others to see if it would be advisable to put his name before congress as a candidate for president. They unanimously agreed that "for the sake of the peace and integrity of Colombia it was advisable that the Liberator should not be re-elected by Congress, but that, if the electoral college to meet next October gave him their votes, he should accept." Caicedo, Herrán, and Luis Baralt were given the unpleasant task of delivering this opinion to Bolívar, who could not control his anger.

On April 27, 1830, Bolívar wrote his last message to

congress. "The common good of the fatherland demands my separation from the country that has given me life in order that my presence may not prove a hindrance to the well-being of my compatriots." That same day Turner and Colonel Patrick Campbell visited Bolívar, who informed them that "he was thoroughly disgusted by the changeable and capricious character of his countrymen and by the calumnies undeservedly heaped upon him, . . . that the restored dominion of Spain, however despotic and tyrannical, would be a blessing to South America by ensuring tranquility, and that he bitterly rued the hour at which he ever thought the Colombians worthy of being freed from it."

In May the congress elected Mosquera president, and although Bolívar and others were certain he would refuse, he accepted the office. Bolívar was informed that the decree conferring extraordinary powers on him had been canceled. He replied that he was withdrawing to private life. Crowds in the streets cheered Bolívar's downfall; even more painful to him were the vivas for Santander.

Congress revived the decree of 1823 granting Bolívar 30,000 pesos annually for life, but since the treasury was empty, he was obliged to sell his jewelry and his horses, which brought only 17,000 pesos. On learning of Bolívar's intention to leave Colombia, the Venezuelan troops in the country mutinied and marched home, an act for which he was blamed. Actually, he and his friends were now in danger in Bogotá, for there was no one to protect them against attack.

The night of May 7 was Bolívar's last in Bogotá. Fears of assassination attempts against him were so great that the ministers spent the entire night with him and in the morning accompanied him on the start of his journey to the coast. Instead of taking Manuela with him, he wrote her affectionately, warning her to be discreet, and promising to send for her when he had decided on his final destination. It seems likely that he did not take her because he expected to return to Bogotá soon. Sucre, misinformed by Bolívar as to the time of his departure (probably to avoid a painful farewell), sent a letter by courier. "You know," he said, "that it is not your power but your friendship that inspired in me the tenderest affection to your person."

"If it gave you pain to write to me," Bolívar replied, "what shall I say, who leave not only my friends, but my country."

Bolívar traveled slowly toward Cartagena, keeping informed daily of events in Bogotá. As a politician he had failed, for his ideas differed too greatly from those of the men in the nations he had made independent. None of them was eager to be a part of any multination organization, for rivalries and jealousies took precedence over goals such as unity and stability. It was no coincidence that Bolívar's departure from power and the collapse of Gran Colombia were almost simultaneous.

On May 22 the new constitution was read on the steps of the cathedral in Bogotá while the citizens looked on with apathy or indifference. Earlier constitutions had caused great excitement and expectation, but the original belief that constitutions could work miracles had been replaced by cynicism.

As he rode toward the coast, Bolívar pondered the failure of his life's work; it was simply that the distance between his plans and what could be accomplished was far too wide to be easily bridged. His analysis of what was wrong politically was accurate, but his remedies were rejected and discredited. Even as he presumably headed for exile abroad, he could not help thinking about a summons from Bogotá to return to power once more to save the fatherland.

NINE

The Liberator's Last Days

UNDECIDED AS TO whether he should retire to one of the Caribbean islands, where he would be available if called on, or to turn his back on Colombia and seek a haven in Europe, thereby admitting to himself that his ungrateful countrymen would never recall him, Bolívar traveled slowly down the Magdalena. As was his custom, he bathed daily in cold springs along the way. When one of his companions recalled that Alexander the Great had died after bathing, Bolívar smiled. "When Alexander went into a cold bath, all flushed," he replied, "he was at the peak of his glory. Such danger does not exist for me. Besides," he added bitterly, "some attribute his death to Antipater, who poisoned him, as Santander tried to murder me."

Bolívar's friends in Bogotá were greatly agitated by his departure, for their well-being and safety had depended largely upon him. They were unhappy that Mosquera, not General Caicedo, had been elected chief executive, for they knew that they could control Caicedo. Mosquera, on the other hand, was more arrogant than passive, and they feared that any influence they had over him was ephemeral.

In May Bolívar reached Turbaco, physically weak and depressed, though the warm and respectful welcome he received there raised his spirits and revived him temporarily. He wrote Caicedo, "I shall not be surprised if a thousand follies are committed, and if they are attributed to me."

As he expected, when he had not gone far from Bogotá his enemies attacked Manuela, who defended herself with her customary verve. She and Urdaneta worked tirelessly to undermine and overthrow the government of Mosquera and Caicedo so that Bolívar would be recalled. She sent her servants to distribute broadsides demanding that Bolívar be returned to power; statements such as "Viva Bolívar, Founder of the Republic!" mysteriously appeared on walls throughout Bogotá. As the attacks on her intensified, the women of Bogotá rallied to her defense for the first time.

Manuela still guarded several trunks full of Bolívar's private papers. Dr. Azuero, out of prison or returned from exile, and now in the council as minister of the interior, demanded that she surrender them to the government. She refused. Azuero also urged the government to expel her from the country. Stubbornly she remained in Bogotá, determined to see Bolívar once more ruler of Colombia.

When a broadside entitled "The Tower of Babel" — a bold attack on the government for its weakness — appeared in Bogotá, a judge ordered alderman Domingo Durán to arrest her. Forewarned, she was in bed, presumably ill, and Durán happily and chivalrously withdrew. The judge sent him back to arrest her, ill or not. She seemed to have recovered quickly from her ailments, for she met Durán at the top of the stairs, sword in hand, ready to defend herself. Once more Durán retreated.

A crowd had gathered to watch the fun, and it saw the mayor, the judge, a detachment of troops, and about half of the city police attempt to arrest one unprotected woman. When they broke into her house they looked up into the barrels of two cocked pistols Manuela pointed at them, and once more the government's prestige was in serious jeopardy.

Bolívar's friend Pepe Paris arrived and negotiated a compromise: Manuela would surrender to restore what remained of the government's dignity. Once the arrest was made she would be immediately freed. It was a temporary victory for Manuela, and it contributed to the government's downfall.

Not satisfied with ridding themselves of the "tyrant" Bolívar, his enemies met to plot Sucre's murder as well, for he was Bolívar's political heir. General Santamaría, one of the group that plotted Sucre's destruction, wrote a friend that as he left the meeting, "I came across Sucre, who was pacing the forecourt of the Cathedral with crossed arms. I was shocked, as if I had seen a ghost, having just decreed his death."

Sucre, who still desired only to return to private life on his wife's estate in Quito, was preparing to return there. General Caicedo, knowing there were plots against Sucre's life, and that General Flores had declared Ecuador independent of Gran Colombia, cautioned him to leave immediately and to go by sea because of his enemies in Pasto. His friends also begged him to take another route, but he laughed at their fears. Like Bolívar, he could not believe that anyone would want to kill him. On the day he rode out of Bogotá, however, the conspirators sent a courier ahead of him to alert Obando that Sucre was coming.

On June 1, the liberal Bogotá newspaper *El Demócrata* published a vicious attack on Sucre, ending with the ominous hope that "perhaps Obando will do to Sucre what we failed to do to Bolívar." Three days later, as Sucre rode through a narow pass in the Berrueco Mountains, hidden men sent by Obando and José Hilario López shot him down. Soon after this, López was promoted to general as a reward for his part in the assassination.

In Venezuela the former guerrilla chief José Yáñez led a movement against Bolívar, in a crude attempt to pressure Colombia into forcibly exiling him. The Venezuelan congress, in a poorly disguised effort to achieve the same purpose, informed Mosquera that it was still "ready to enter into relations and transactions" with Colombia, but "taught by a number of evils of all kinds to be prudent, and seeing in General Simón Bolívar the origin of these evils . . . protests that such relations cannot be engaged in while he remains in the territory of Colombia."

In his reply to the Venezuelan government, Minister of the Interior Azuero simply emphasized the importance of the negotiations and future relations between the two countries. He sent the Venezuelan note and his reply to Bolívar, commenting that the president was very much embarrassed by the situation and could not decide what action to take. Mosquera instructed Azuero to delay any action for the moment, but Azuero released for publication the Venezuelan note, his reply to it, and his letter to Bolívar. This was clearly an act of insubordination, but Mosquera supinely failed to dismiss Azuero or even to reprimand him. "I assure you," Bolívar said to a friend, "that this is the event of my life which has affected me most deeply."

Dr. Azuero also took inhuman pleasure in sending Bolívar news of Sucre's death. "My God!" Bolívar exclaimed. "They have shed the blood of Abel. It is impossible to live in a country where the most famous generals are cruelly and barbarously murdered, the very men to whom America owes its freedom. . . . I believe the purpose of the crime was to deprive the fatherland of my successor. I can no longer live in such a country." He asked to be alone, and paced nervously back and forth in the patio until late at night, then rose at dawn and resumed his pacing. As a result he caught a chill and fever that continued until his death.

Deeply depressed over his personal loss and the extreme anarchy and base treachery the murder reflected, Bolívar wanted to leave for Europe and forget the past. Montilla and other friends urged him to stay. Bolívar remained, torn between the desire to leave the ungrateful country and the undying hope that he would be called on to save the fatherland once more. Daily he expected to receive the news that his friends had forced Mosquera and Caicedo from power.

Although there were violent expressions of hatred of Bolívar in Caracas, where he had been declared outlaw, and in Bogotá, the people of Quito invited him to live among them, and Bolivia was willing to name him ambassador to the Vatican. He still had friends among the Venezuelan officers, and a group of them petitioned him to help preserve Colombian unity and offered him the presidency, which was not rightly theirs to dispose.

As president, Mosquera had been received with apathy rather than enthusiasm, and he did nothing to discourage the men who had been exiled or imprisoned after the September 25 attack on Bolívar from returning to Bogotá and meddling in politics. Both Gómez and Azuero had, in fact, been named to the council of ministers. Mosquera apparently feared Santander and his supporters more than Bolívar and his friends.

As Manuela and Urdaneta plotted for Bolívar's return, the ineffectiveness of the government daily increased their following. The conviction was spreading that Bolívar alone had the power and prestige necessary to pacify the country and preserve order. From Jamaica O'Leary and Belford

Wilson carried on a propaganda campaign against the government of Mosquera and Caicedo.

Late in July the Boyacá regiment, which opposed Bolívar's return, marched into Bogotá with shouts of "Death to Urdaneta" and vivas for Santander. Soon after this the government ordered the Callao regiment to transfer its garrison from Bogotá to Tunja, for it was composed of veterans of Junín and Ayacucho who were intensely loyal to Bolívar. Friends of Bolívar deluged the government with protests that if the Callao regiment left the city it would be an invitation to the "liberals" and the Boyacá regiment to destroy them. Mosquera was out of the city, and Azuero and José Ignacio Márquez rejected the petitions and ordered the Callao regiment to march at once. The regiment, commanded by a Colonel Johnson, went a short distance from the city and then demanded the dismissal of Azuero and other ministers.

Caicedo was willing to comply, but the Santander faction was not. While Mosquera negotiated with the rebels, the government brought up reinforcements. Azuero drafted an unacceptable amnesty decree, which Mosquera timidly signed. Urdaneta, who was trying to calm the government and encourage rebellion at the same time so as to be able to seize power himself, urged the rebels to reject the amnesty. They routed a force the government sent against them and Mosquera capitulated, agreeing to exile Azuero, Márquez, and twelve of Santander's other men. The rebel regiment marched into Bogotá but committed no acts of violence. Mosquera named Urdaneta minister of war, and a number of cities proclaimed Bolívar president.

Bolívar received dozens of letters from friends urging him to return, and the ambassadors of Britain, Brazil, and the United States openly declared that no one else could save Colombia. The military and civil authorities of Cartagena named him chief of the army and assured him of complete freedom of action.

Early in September Mosquera and Caicedo resigned, as Bolívar had anticipated. He wrote Urdaneta, assuring him of his support, but when Urdaneta's commission arrived in Cartagena to invite him to return and assume the presidency, he declined. "I am old, ill, tired, disappointed, grieved, calumniated, and badly paid," he said. "Believe me, I have never looked upon insurrections with friendly eyes, and during these last days I have even repented of those we undertook against the Spaniards." He concluded, "All my reasoning comes to the same conclusion: I have no hope of saving the fatherland."

For the first time in his life Bolívar's rejection of power offered him was definite and sincere, for nothing had any meaning for him — everything he had attempted had ended in futility. He despaired for his beloved America. "How could anyone imagine," he asked bitterly, "that a whole world could fall into the frenzy of devouring its own kith and kin like cannibals?"

By mid-October Bolívar's health was much worse, and he was wracked by a chronic cough. He went to Barranquilla in a vain search for a place that could restore his health. Despite his increasing weakness, he continued his daily letter writing. At Montilla's suggestion, Joaquín de Mier, a Spaniard and former royalist, offered Bolívar his country house on the hacienda of San Pedro Alejandrino near Santa Marta. Bolívar delayed several weeks before accepting the offer, meanwhile sending Montilla and Urdaneta advice he had found "on my sad pillow." Though his health was gone his mind was clear and his thoughts were as logical as ever.

In November he wrote Montilla concerning communications from the rebels Flores in Ecuador and José Domingo Espinar in Panama. "What is absolutely certain," he said, "is that the populations of both places are among the most devoted to me. . . . It is hoped with good reason that on my answers being received everything will end happily." The two caudillos were in the process of carving out domains for themselves, however, and all did not end as Bolívar expected.

One of his companions, José Vallarino, reported on a conversation he had with Bolívar at this time.

> We spoke about the political state of Colombia. "The peoples," he said, "are tired and want nothing but peace and order; to think that liberal ideas are general is a mistake; many wise people are against the representative system for they think it does not fit these countries." I argued that a new people could adopt any kind of constitution, so long as it was firmly maintained for long enough for the people to become used to it; "Do not believe it," he retorted with liveliness. "Here men are used to the Spanish system, and there is no power strong enough to run contrary to habits rooted in the heart."

To Flores Bolívar sent the few conclusions he had reached after holding power for twenty years: America is ungovernable. He who serves a revolution plows the sea. The only thing one can do in America is to emigrate. The country will inevitably fall into the hands of an unbridled crowd of petty tyrants almost too small for notice and of all colors and races. There were others, all reflecting his bitterness.

Early in December a French physician, Dr. Alexandre Prosper Révérend, visited Bolívar at the San Pedro Alejandrino hacienda and stayed by his side the remaining days of his life. He diagnosed Bolívar's illness as the advanced stage of tuberculosis, for which there was no cure. Even if there had been a remedy, however, in his depressed state of mind Bolívar would have refused all medicines.

On one occasion he asked Dr. Révérend why he had come to America. "For the sake of liberty," he replied.

"And have you found it here?"

"Certainly, Your Excellency."

"Ah, then you have been more fortunate than I. . . ."

On December 10 the Bishop of Santa Marta visited Bolívar, and after talking to the physician urged Bolívar to put his affairs in order. Apparently for the first time Bolívar realized that there was no hope of recovery. He immediately drew up his will and ordered all papers that might be used to discredit Urdaneta and his government burned. On December 11 he wrote Briceño, pleading with him to become reconciled with Urdaneta, for "only by sacrificing our personal feelings can we protect our friends and Colombia from the horrors of anarchy." Many times in the past Bolívar himself had been forced to sacrifice his own feelings for the sake of independence.

At one o'clock on the afternoon of December 17, 1830 — the same month, day, and hour that eleven years earlier he had signed the agreement uniting Venezuela and New Granada to create Gran Colombia — Bolívar breathed his last. When it was discovered that he had nothing in his wardrobe but shabby and worn clothing, General José Laurencio Silva came to the rescue. The Liberator of Venezuela, Colombia, Ecuador, Peru, and Bolivia was buried in a borrowed shirt.

Epilogue

AT THE TIME of his death Bolívar was revered by those who were still loyal to him and was intensely hated by partisans of Santander and Páez. Some American diplomatic agents, who undoubtedly felt obliged to denounce anyone whose name was linked with monarchy, expressed themselves freely on this subject, and their view of Bolívar was largely unfavorable. Several foreign officers who had served with Bolívar and then had been alienated from him wrote uncomplimentary books about him. In 1829, however, Martin Van Buren took a more temperate view when he commented: "Public opinion will not require for the Libertador . . . more than the actual conditions his country will allow. It is well known that circumstances, which are the results of centuries, cannot be overcome in an hour. The world will, therefore, give him full credit for advising . . . the establishment of institutions as liberal as existing circumstances will permit."

When the Mosquera-Caicedo government resigned and Urdaneta took over control of the country, he and Manuela had written and waited in vain for Bolívar's reply that he was returning to Bogotá. Finally Manuela had set out to rejoin him and, hopefully, to accompany him on a triumphal reentry into Bogotá. She had reached Honda, the river port at the upper end of navigation on the Magdalena, where she was preparing to take a riverboat downstream, when a messenger brought the news that Bolívar had died. Sadly she retraced her steps to Bogotá, a nest of his enemies as well as a haven for his friends. "When he lived," Manuela declared, "I loved Bolívar. Dead, I venerate him."

Santander remained abroad until 1832, when, under a new constitution, he was elected president. Manuela's friends pleaded with her to seek safety in some other land, but she stubbornly remained in Bogotá until January, 1834, when Santander ordered her to leave the country within three days. Manuela ignored the order, but Santander sent her under guard to the dungeons of Cartagena, where he had been held after the attempt to assassinate Bolívar. She remained in a gloomy cell for several months, then was placed on a British ship bound for Jamaica, where Bolívar's old friend Maxwell Hyslop came to her rescue.

In the spring of 1835 Manuela wrote General Flores, then dictator of Ecuador, mentioning letters from him to Bolívar among the papers in her possession. Flores sent her a passport, but by the time she reached Guayaquil he was temporarily out of power, and she was not allowed to return to her native Quito. She took a ship to the Peruvian port village of Paita, a favorite stopping place for American whalers about to sail across the Pacific. Among her visitors were Herman Melville, Giuseppe Garibaldi, and eighty-year-old Simón Rodríguez. Unable to recover any of her property from Bogotá, and denied the 8,000 pesos — the amount of her dowry — left her by Dr. Thorne as his legacy to her, she lived in poverty, eking out a living by the sale of sweets.

For twelve years Bolívar's remains were interred in Santa Marta. Santander died in 1840, and in 1842 the Republic of Venezuela began to atone for the injustices done Bolívar in his last years by sending a commission to exhume his remains and take them to Caracas. Commissioners of Venezuela and New Granada, accompanied by a great crowd of people, including civil and ecclesiastical officials, naval officers from warships sent by England, France, and Holland, and Dr. Alexandre Prosper Révérend, who had stayed at Bolívar's side during his final illness, disinterred his coffin while naval cannons roared and priests intoned funeral chants. The Venezuelan warship *Constitución*, escorted by the foreign warships, carried the coffin to La Guaira. In Caracas Bolívar's remains were again honored, and some of his old friends carried his catafalque through the streets to the cathedral.

Bolívar's faithful aide O'Leary returned to Caracas in 1833, then for six years served as secretary of the Venezuelan legation in England and Europe. In 1835, accompanied by his brother-in-law, General Soublette, he visited General Pablo Morillo in La Coruña. Learning that O'Leary was writing a life story of his old rival, whom he greatly admired, Morillo gave him many documents the royalists had captured in battles. In 1840 O'Leary returned to Caracas, where he participated in the ceremonies held when Bolívar's remains were brought home. In 1844 he became British consul general in Bogotá, where he continued writing his memoirs of his years with the Liberator. He corresponded with Manuela, who answered his questions in detail and told him where she had hidden some of Bolívar's letters in Bogotá. O'Leary retrieved the letters and sent them to her by courier. Before his sudden death in Bogotá in 1854, he had completed his memoirs in two volumes, to which he added twelve more volumes of Bolívar's letters, and fourteen of documents. A final volume was on Bolívar's relationship with Manuela, but the Venezuelan government suppressed it. By this time Bolívar was acknowledged a national hero of Venezuela and New Granada, and none of his admirers except O'Leary would admit that Manuela had existed. When other men began writing eulogistic biographies of Bolívar they did not even mention her name, and a box of papers concerning her mysteriously disappeared from the Bogotá archives.

In 1856 a sailor who had contracted diphtheria went ashore in Paita, and soon the dread disease became epidemic. Manuela, who had broken her hip earlier, was unable to move to safety and succumbed to the disease. She was buried in a common grave with dozens of other victims of the epidemic, and local officials burned all of her possessions, including the trunks of Bolívar's papers and her letters from him, which she had guarded for a quarter of a century.

The bitterness against Bolívar gradually subsided. Páez, who had turned his countrymen against him, admitted in his autobiography, completed in the 1860s: "Simón Bolívar belongs to the band of modern men whose equals are to be found only when we reach back to the republican times of Greece and Rome. . . . In the midst of people who had no more tradition than the respect for an authority sanctioned by the acquiescence of three centuries of ignorance, superstition, and fanaticism, nor any political dogma but submission to an order of things supported by might and force, Bolívar succeeded in defying that power."

As a means of stimulating civic pride, the Venezuelan government in 1852 established the *Busto del Libertador* (Bust of the Liberator), to be awarded to eminent and deserving individuals of any nation. After 1872 President

Antonio Guzmán Blanco made the major effort to restore Bolívar's reputation; when the National Pantheon was established in a former church in Caracas, he had Bolívar's remains placed in it, along with those of other national heroes. He proclaimed Bolívar's birthday a national holiday, staged the lavish Bolívar centennial celebrations in 1883, and had busts or statues of the Liberator placed in town plazas all over the country. The *Academia Venezolana Correspondiente a la Real Española* was created, also as part of the centennial celebrations, and a marble statue of the Liberator by Italian sculptor Pietro Tenerani was placed in the National Pantheon. All of the countries Bolívar had liberated also celebrated the centennial of his birth, and Tenerani produced a bronze statue of Bolívar for Bogotá. In 1910, the centennial of the independence movement, a bronze equestrian statue of Bolívar by the French sculptor Manuel Frémiet was placed in Independence Park, Bogotá. In 1921 an equestrian statue of Bolívar by the American sculptor James Farnham was set up in Central Park, New York City.

By the twentieth century Bolívar had become the favorite subject of writers all over Spanish America, and a common practice was to compare him to some national hero such as Morelos of Mexico. A favorite topic of Argentine and Venezuelan writers has been the controversial, undocumented meeting between Bolívar and San Martín in Guayaquil. An enormous amount of hero-worshipping literature has appeared, but there have also been many serious studies of Bolívar's role as educator, promoter of abolition of slavery, and especially as proponent of Spanish-American confederation and hemispheric solidarity. Books extolling Bolívar have been published in a number of European countries as well as in the United States. A bibliography of works on Bolívar found mainly in the Library of the Pan American Union and the Library of

Congress in 1930 filled nineteen pages, and it was admittedly far from complete.

Since the establishment of the Pan American Union in 1890 (known as the International Bureau of American Republics until 1910), Bolívar's name has always been linked to the promotion of internationalism or Pan-Americanism. Others may have had somewhat similar ideas before him, but Bolívar provided the only sustained effort to bring about the Congress of Panama in 1826. Although its work had proved disappointing to him, it was the first major step toward a union of American states.

In June, 1926, the Pan-American Centennial Congress met in Panama to celebrate Bolívar's services in the cause of American confederation and continental solidarity. Dr. Charles W. Hackett, a member of the United States delegation, expressed the views of many in his address, "Bolívar's Title to Immortality."

"While Bolívar's greatest achievement was the liberation of a major region imperial in extent," Hackett said,

> that work, great as it was, fails by far to constitute his sole contribution to posterity. His prophetic vision of Panama as the seat of an "august congress" is clearly revealed in the Jamaica letter; his political philosophy is best set forth in the Angostura address and in the first Constitution of Bolivia. Moreover — himself a man of education and culture — Bolívar found time despite his multifarious and stupendous duties on the field of battle and in the council halls, to promote education. In his address to the Congress of Angostura Bolívar made the following pronouncement that is worthy of being a motto of any free people:
>
> "Popular education must be the paramount care of the paternal love of Congress. Morals and enlightenment are the poles of a republic; morals and enlightenment are our prime necessities."

Today Bolívar is venerated for his enormous sacrifices as patriot and general and is recognized for his roles as protagonist of a strong centralized government and as promoter of Spanish-American cooperation. His disillusion with both political radicalism and democracy have been stressed by many of his biographers. Recently, however, a revisionist work* suggests that Bolívar was a liberal and realistic democrat as well as a farsighted reformer who had sought social and economic reforms such as abolition of slavery, administrative reorganization, and (on unconvincing evidence) redistribution of land. Books about some facet of Bolívar's life and career are still being published, for the Liberator has become an inexhaustible theme. So far, however, there has been no attempt to downgrade his achievements. When he lived, he was willing for history to judge him on the basis of the record, and history has placed him first among Spanish-American heroes.

* J. L. Salcedo-Bastardo, *Visión y revisión de Bolívar,* 3rd ed. (Caracas, 1957).

Suggested Readings

THERE ARE LITERALLY hundreds of books on Bolívar. A few of the best in English are:

Salvador de Madariaga, *Bolívar* (New York: Pellegrini and Cudahy, 1952).

Gerhard Masur, *Simón Bolívar* (Albuquerque: University of New Mexico Press, 1948).

Robert F. McNerney, Jr., tr. and ed., *Bolívar and the War of Independence. Memorias del General Daniel Florencio O'Leary. Narración* (abridged version) (Austin: University of Texas Press, 1970).

Luis B. Prieto, *Simón Bolívar: Educator* (Garden City: Doubleday and Co., 1970).

Victor Wolfgang von Hagen, *The Four Seasons of Manuela: The Love Story of Manuela Sáenz and Simón Bolívar* (New York: Duell, Sloan and Pearce, 1952).

T. R. Ybarra, *Bolívar, the Passionate Warrior* (New York: Ives and Washburn, 1929).

Index